CULTURES OF THE WORLD®

SOMALIA

Susan M. Hassig & Zawiah Abdul Latif

Marshall Cavendish
Benchmark
New York

PICTURE CREDITS

Cover photo: © Michael S. Yamashita/Corbis

alt.TYPE / Reuters: 36, 54 • Andes Press Agency: 90, 96, 103 • Audrius Tomonis: 135 • Barnaby's Picture Library: 79, 81, 94 • Corbis: 86 • Eye Ubiquitous / Hutchison: 47, 50, 61, 92, 120, 125 • Hulton-Deutsch: 19, 20, 24 • Hutchison: 9, 14, 21, 37, 39, 58, 68, 73, 75, 80, 87, 91, 99, 100, 101, 106, 111, 117, 119 • Image Bank: 13, 15 • Bjorn Klingwall: 12, 27, 31, 42, 77, 104, 105, 108, 115, 121, 122, 124, 127 • Jason Laure: 44, 102, 112, 113 • Lonely Planet Images: 5, 6, 18, 28, 93 • National Geographic Image Collection: 7, 48, 62 • R. Ian Lloyd / Marka: 131 • R. Ian Lloyd / STOCKFOOD: 130 • Reuters / Visnews Library: 8, 30 • Liba Taylor: 3, 4, 7, 16, 38, 41, 55, 56, 59, 60, 63, 64, 65, 67, 69, 71, 74, 84, 85, 88, 97, 109, 118, 122, 126, 129

PRECEDING PAGE

Smiling Somali girls in a village near Baidoa.

Publisher (U.S.): Michelle Bisson
Editors: Deborah Grahame, Mabelle Yeo, Crystal Ouyang, Kim Siang Yong
Copyreader: Daphne Hougham
Designers: Jailani Basari, Rachel Chen
Cover picture researcher: Connie Gardner
Picture researchers: Thomas Khoo, Joshua Ang

Marshall Cavendish Benchmark
99 White Plains Road
Tarrytown, NY 10591
Web site: www.marshallcavendish.us

© Times Editions Private Limited 1996
© Marshall Cavendish International (Asia) Private Limited 2008
All rights reserved. First edition 1996. Second edition 2008.
® "Cultures of the World" is a registered trademark of Times Publishing Limited.

Originated and designed by Times Editions
An imprint of Marshall Cavendish International (Asia) Private Limited
A member of Times Publishing Limited

All Internet sites were correct and accurate at the time of printing. All monetary figures in this publication are in U.S. dollars.

Library of Congress Cataloging-in-Publication Data
Hassig, Susan M., 1969–
    Somalia/by Susan M. Hassig & Zawiah Abdul Latif. — 2nd ed.
       p. cm. — (Cultures of the world)
    Summary: "Provides comprehensive information on the geography, history, wildlife, governmental structure, economy, cultural diversity, peoples, religion, and culture of Somalia." — Provided by publisher.
    Includes bibliographical references and index.
       ISBN 978-0-7614-2082-8
    1. Somalia—Juvenile literature. I. Latif, Zawiah Abdul. II. Title. III. Series
    CT401.5.H37 2007
    967.73—dc22   2006102270

Printed in China

9 8 7 6 5 4 3 2 1

CONTENTS

A girl wearing a typical Somali headscarf.

A Somali boy selling coconuts.

INTRODUCTION

ALONG THE EASTERN COAST OF AFRICA lies the peninsula the ancient Egyptians called "God's Land." Part of it is Somalia—a nation deeply united by kinship yet divided by blood. It is home to over 8.8 million people bound together by a common culture, ancestry, and religion. Yet a bloody civil war still rages as Somalis fight one another for political and territorial control. The Somali nomads follow a way of life that dates back centuries. They also have a rich oral literary tradition and are especially well known for their poetry.

After years under the colonial yoke, Somalia gained its independence from Great Britain and Italy in 1960. The dominant rule of Siad Barre from 1969 to 1991, and the collapse of a central government thereafter, left Somalia undone by factional fighting and anarchy for the next two decades. Today Somalia is struggling to make a success of its fourteenth attempt to establish a government since 1991. The people of Somalia have endured the difficult years of colonialism, tyranny, civil war, and famine with a fierce, indomitable spirit. Perhaps in the near future, with additional international support and aid, Somalis can finally heal themselves and rise above their deep political division to define the destiny of their country.

GEOGRAPHY

SOMALIA'S STRETCH OF COASTLINE is about 2,422 miles (3,898 km) long. It is washed by the Indian Ocean on the east, with the Gulf of Aden to the north. Over the centuries many settlers, including immigrants from the Middle East and elsewhere, have come to Somalia through its coastal towns.

The country's total land area is 242,216 square miles (627,337 square km), about the same size as Texas. To Somalia's west and northwest lies Ethiopia, to its southwest is Kenya, and in the north is the Republic of Djibouti. The four countries of Somalia, Ethiopia, Eritrea, and Djibouti make up the Horn of Africa.

Above: **Ocean waves pound the rocks near the capital of Mogadishu.**

Opposite: **The hot and dry landscape found in Woqooyi Galbeed, Somalia's northwestern region, supports little plant life.**

The terrain of Somalia consists mainly of plains and plateaus, with rugged mountains in the northeast. Coastal plains extend from the lava fields of Djibouti to the southern coastal tip of Somalia. This region, called the Guban, which means "burned from lack of water," lives up to its name. It is a hot and dry area with very little rainfall or vegetation. Superficial and sand-filled watercourses traverse these coastal plains. During the rainy seasons, the watercourses flow toward the sea and vegetation begins to sprout alongside. This enables the nomads to use the region for grazing their herds. Inland from the coast, the plains are dominated by the steep northeastern mountains. The fertile area between the two main rivers, the Jubba and the Shabelle, is another main geographical region.

MOUNTAINS AND RIVERS

Two mountain ranges—the Oogo and the Golis—rise in the northeast region of Somalia. These rugged ranges extend westward and reach an altitude of 9,000 feet (2,743 m) at the city of Harar in Ethiopia. At Harar, the Oogo and the Golis merge with the Ethiopian highlands. Somalia's northeast mountains are magnificent but dangerously precipitous, with altitudes between 5,900 and 6,890 feet (1,798 and 2,100 m) above sea level. Extending south from Ethiopia, the mountains level out and become Somalia's central plateau. Annual rainfall in these ranges often exceeds 20 inches (50.8 cm).

In the southwest, the Jubba and the Shabelle rivers flow from Ethiopia through southern Somalia, carving out expansive valleys rich with vegetation. The Jubba River spills into the Indian Ocean at the town of

The semibarren areas of the north become deserts during the hottest periods of the year.

Kismaayo in the south. The Shabelle River winds from Ethiopia toward the town of Balcad, about 20 miles (32.2 km) north of the capital, Mogadishu.

Unlike the rest of the country, the fertile area between the two main rivers supported farms and plantations even before Somalia was under colonial rule. Today, verdant grasslands, forests, and wildlife still depend on these rivers.

THE CENTRAL PLATEAU

The Haud extends from four corners—the city of Hargeysa (northwest), the city of Galcaio (northeast), the Doollo plains (west), and the Nugaal valley (east). This central region at one time supported lush vegetation and lakes during the rainy seasons, and Somali nomads would move into the area. But since there is no permanent water source, the herdsmen would be gone again during the dry season. In recent times, with mechanized wells dug and water reservoirs created, the nomads and herdsmen do not have to move away in search of water sources.

Because the Haud extends into Ethiopia, Somalis and Ethiopians have been in conflict over the rights to pasture in this area since the 1960s, with Somalia still claiming sovereignty over the region. Under an earlier agreement, Ethiopia had allowed British Somaliland migrants to pasture in its own part of the Haud, but when Somalia gained independence from the British in 1960, Ethiopia no longer wanted to extend this right.

These Somalis are pleased to find a water-hole in the area between the Jubba and Shabelle rivers for their cattle.

THE SELF-DECLARED REPUBLIC OF SOMALILAND

In 1991 the people of the northern region declared themselves independent from Somalia, calling their new state the Republic of Somaliland. This self-declared nation extends 400 miles (644 km) east of Djibouti, with the Gulf of Aden to the north. As of 2005, an estimated 3.5 million people lived in Somaliland.

This northern region was a British protectorate from 1887. It was briefly captured by the Italians at the start of World War II, but the British reclaimed it toward the end of the war. When Somalia obtained independence from colonial rule in 1960, the former British protectorate joined it to form the United Republic of Somalia.

In the late 1970s, as result of the dictatorial nature of Siad Barre's regime, armed opposition groups formed across the border in Ethiopia. One of these, the Somali National Front, led the northern region to secession from Somalia when the Barre regime fell in 1991. Thus, the northerners declared their independence from Somalia and selected their own head of state. In 1993 Somaliland's interim legislature replaced its first head of state with a new president, Mohammed Ibrahim Egal.

Today Somaliland has a republican form of government headed by an elected president, a legislative assembly, and an independent judiciary. The country also has its own police force and currency. Somaliland's first multiparty presidential election, held in 2003, was won by incumbent leader Dahir Riyale Kahin, who was appointed president in 2002 following the death of Egal.

Somaliland's sovereignty is not recognized internationally, and it is still regarded as part of Somalia.

CLIMATE

In precolonial and colonial Somalia times, the climate was continuously hot and dry except during the main rainy season from April to June which was favorable for vegetation and grazing pastures. This three-month season was important to farmers and nomads as well as Somalis in general. The seasonal rains provided relief from the hot and dry weather and allowed people to observe religious ceremonies, get married, renew contracts, or negotiate disputes.

At that time, many Somalis calculated their age by the number of April to June wet seasons they had lived through.

The other rainy spell was shorter and lasted only two months, from October to November, and accounted for about 30 percent of the annual rainfall then.

The colonial boundaries drawn up by the previous foreign administrations in Somalia affected the Somali-inhabited areas that were being cut off from one another. With the passage of time, commercial livestock rearing as well as population expansion also crept in. These, perhaps, contributed to some parts of Somalia becoming desert wastelands today.

Somalia currently experiences seasonal monsoon winds. The northeast monsoon lasts from December to February. In the middle part of the year, from May to October, southwest monsoons occur. Somalis have accustomed themselves to an irregular annual rainfall. This irregularity may have been the reason for recurring droughts in recent times. In between the monsoon periods, the weather in Somalia is hot and humid.

SPARSE VEGETATION

Due to the irregular rainfall, vegetation is rather sparse in Somalia except for the areas along the Jubba and Shabelle rivers. Trees native to the dry highlands are the boswellia and commiphora. Frankincense and myrrh, renowned since biblical times, are the aromatic products of these trees.

In most of the country, low trees such as acacia cover patches of short grass, desert, and sand dunes. The mountainous region, though, supports a wider variety of vegetation, including aloe plants and remnants of juniper forests at altitudes exceeding 4,920 feet (1,500 m).

The steep mountains of Somalia rise in the northeast, reaching their highest point of 7,900 feet (2,408 m) at Surud Ad.

The bizarre sight of a towering termites' nest reaching nearly as high as a tree.

SOMALI WILDLIFE

Somalia is rich in biodiversity. A number of different kinds of animal species as well as plant life are found exclusively there.

On the Somali plains are enormous termite mounds that look like small hills. These towering nests are solid structures of hard-baked earth, formed and glued together by the insects' saliva and droppings. They are quite a sight to behold.

The larger mammals are the lion, cheetah, leopard, elephant, buffalo, zebra, giraffe, and hippopotamus. Male lions that roam the central region can exceed 9 feet (2.7 m) in length and have either black or tawny manes.

The cheetah, the fastest mammal on earth, has a golden or gray coat with black spots and a white belly. Hunters have viciously killed off all the rhinoceroses in Somalia and most of east Africa, and even the elephant is in danger of being wiped out.

Also in Somalia's semiarid regions donkeys, sheep, gazelles, giraffes, and antelopes can be found. The species of giraffe native to Somalia is the reticulated giraffe. It has a reddish brown coat on which there are large smooth-edged geometric patches and has either two or three horns.

Small antelopes known as dik-diks live in the north and along the Jubba and Shabelle rivers. The name dik-dik comes from the sound made by the animal, which is only 12 inches (30 cm) high at the shoulders, with a soft, gray coat. The male has small horns often covered by a patch of hair. The dik-dik is the emblem of the Somali police.

The pink flamingo and the hoopoe are among Somalia's most colorful birds. The hoopoe has pinkish brown feathers with black-and-white stripes. Its crested head was featured in many ancient Egyptian drawings.

The hoopoe used to have a golden crest, according to Somali storytellers. But these bright African birds begged King Solomon to change their crests to a chestnut shade because too many hunters were killing them for their gold feathers.

Colorful birds like the pink flamingo are found in the riverine areas of the south.

POETRY OF THE CAMEL

The camel is the most important animal to Somali nomads—so essential, in fact, that many poems and songs have been written about it. In the Somali language, there are 46 different words to describe camels. Traditionally, the noblest occupational calling in Somalia was camel herding. The richer a family became, the more camels it would buy, because a family's standing in the community was often measured by the number of camels it owned.

Somalis not only use camels to transport themselves and their possessions but they also slaughter the animals at some religious occasions. In addition, they exchange camels to symbolize the mending of a broken relationship or for cultivating a friendship.

Camels are indispensable to the Somalis, especially to the nomad, whose livelihoods depend on mobility.

HOW THE LEOPARD GOT ITS SPOTS

The leopard is the symbol of Somalia and appears on government stamps and parade flags.

These lithe and beautiful animals live along the northeast coast, and near the Jubba River, sharing their habitat with lions and cheetahs. Leopards have long been coveted for their hides, but leopard hunting is now prohibited.

Somalis like to tell the story of the leopard and the Ethiopian man. This tale has also been recounted by the English writer Rudyard Kipling.

An Ethiopian man was out hunting one day with a leopard by his side. "You are

an incredible hunter," said the man to the leopard. "The only thing is, all the animals can spot you from miles away. That's because your coat is as bright as a sunflower!"

"Well, do something about it then," said the leopard. "How about putting some spots on my body? That will help me blend in with the foliage. But just make sure you don't make the spots too big, as I have no wish to look like the giraffe."

The Ethiopian smiled and obliged by pressing his fingers to his own dark skin and then pressing his fingertips onto the leopard's skin. Wherever he touched the leopard, there appeared five little marks, close together. Several times the man's fingers slipped, and those marks came out somewhat blurred, blending into one another.

That is why to this day, so say the Somalis, there are always tight clusters of five small black spots on the leopard's coat, and why some black spots look much bigger than the others.

The hippo, which looks harmless enough, may sometimes attack a person venturing into the water. But Somalis run a greater risk from the wild buffalo, which may charge at the slightest disturbance.

A Somali nomad and his herd of goats.

NOMADIC AND TOWN LIFE

Somalia has been called a nation of nomads. Even with modernization, this lifestyle still survives today, practiced by some Somalis.

Scarcity of water sources and irregular rainfall force Somali nomads to be constantly on the move, roaming the country with their flocks of sheep, goats, and camels in search of water as well as new pastures. Once the nomads find a suitable place for a temporary stay, they build makeshift homes with sticks and animal skins that they transport from place to place on the backs of camels or donkeys. Somali nomads themselves often travel with nothing more than the clothes on their backs, a bowl for food or water, a staff for herding, and a headrest for their sleep at night.

They live in the highlands and plateaus during the dry months and migrate to the Haud only during the rainy periods. They set up small temporary settlements in the Haud near dependable sources of water. When the water runs out, nomads return to the highlands until the next rainy season.

The fertile interriverine area between the Jubba and Shabelle rivers has been the site of farming from precolonial times. There, a former slave population exists who suffered exploitation on plantations during the Italian colonial period.

The rest of the Somalis live in small villages scattered throughout the country and in the many towns and cities, often along the eastern coast, facing the Indian Ocean.

MOGADISHU This national capital is the largest Somali city. In the ninth century, Arab and Persian traders founded a colony here, establishing it as a trading port for gold from south central Africa. Its name means "the seat of the shah," a reflection of the Persian influence. Mogadishu continues to serve as a central port for the country. However, the civil war enabled towns and ports in other areas to grow and develop as well.

HARGEYSA Located on a broad plateau in the mountainous north, Hargeysa is an important center for livestock trading. It is also the financial hub for many companies, including retail and food processing. Previously, Hargeysa was the capital of the British protectorate of Somaliland.

KISMAAYO Lying southwest of Mogadishu on the eastern coast, Kismaayo is the third-largest Somali city. It is a major trading center and port. Many of its inhabitants have jobs in industry or fishing.

BERBERA Arab geographers first mentioned this city in the 13th century. It is situated on the northern coast on the Gulf of Aden, and is still an important port, particularly for the export of livestock. It has strong commercial links with Ethiopia, Yemen, and Saudi Arabian ports.

HISTORY

DURING EARLY EGYPTIAN TIMES, Persian, Greek, Roman, and Egyptian seafarers called at Somali coastal ports and loaded their ships with frankincense, myrrh, rhinoceros horns, and ivory. Some of these traveling merchants eventually came to live in this land.

Centuries before, the Somali people themselves were already established inland. Many now believe they are descendants of Muslim immigrants from Arabia who crossed the Red Sea and married indigenous inhabitants of the Horn of Africa. Based on the history of Eastern Cushitic, the Somali language, most scholars believe that Somalis are descendents of people who originated from the area around Lake Tana in Ethiopia.

After the sixth century, foreign traders began settling along the Gulf of Aden. The present town of Zeila was once a walled port town known for its coffee and slave trading. Muslim merchants began to set up homes in Zeila, bringing their religion to the area. By the ninth century, Arab, Persian, and East African traders had founded a colony for handling and shipping gold in what became the city-state of Mogadishu.

Left: **Persian traders of the 14th century. Many Muslim merchants had settled in Somalia by then.**

Opposite: **Ancient rock paintings found at Laas Ga'al, in Mogadishu.**

19

A Persian hunter of the late 14th century. By the 15th century, Muslim settlers in Somalia struggled with the Abyssinian Christians from Ethiopia.

SPREAD OF THE MUSLIM FAITH

The Muslim faith and its cultural beliefs had spread from the coastal towns to the interior by the 14th century because of extensive contact with the Muslim Middle East.

There are some myths about the origins of the major existing clan families in Somalia today. An important Muslim chief, Sheikh Jabarti, from Arabia is thought to have arrived in Somalia in the 11th century. He is believed to have been head of the Darod Somali, a tribal people who were already settled in the northeast corner of the Somali peninsula. In the 13th century, another Muslim leader is said to have been as influential as Sheikh Jabarti. His name was Sheikh Isaq, who is reputed to have founded the Isaq Somali clan.

In the 15th century, the Muslim population became embroiled in a long struggle with Christians from the kingdom of Abyssinia, or present-day Ethiopia. Battles were fought, with Somali tribesmen often forming part of Muslim armies. The relationship between the two lands up to that time had been one of tolerance, because Abyssinian Christians had protected Muslim refugees from Mecca during the seventh century.

An ambitious Abyssinian leader, Yeshaq, successfully invaded a Somali town in 1415. He directed his courtiers to compose a victory hymn, and the song that resulted became the first written record of the name "Somali." Nearly 100 years went by before the Muslims were able to recover from their defeat, but eventually they gathered their forces and invaded the towns of Abyssinia.

Mogadishu flourished in the 13th century and continued to prosper over the next two centuries.

WEALTH OF THE COASTAL TOWNS

Mogadishu first became an urban center in the ninth century. By the 13th century it had become a major town with a Muslim mosque, a theological school, and a palace. The Muslim traveler Ibn Battuta visited in 1331 and recorded that a Somali sultan ruled the city with the aid of ministers, legal experts, and commanders. He also described some of the Mogadishu leaders as eating vast amounts of rich foods.

During the next two centuries, Mogadishu and other coastal trading cities prospered. Inland city-states with strong commerce and trade activities also flourished. The inland sultanate of Ajuuraan that arose is a notable example. It was a loosely structured religious and trade federation, but then internal and external circumstances changed, including the arrival of the Portuguese who interfered with the trade of the East African coast. The Portuguese were eventually ousted, and the southern coast of Somalia (the Banaadir) came under the authority of the sultan of Zanzibar, an island nation south of Somalia. Other European powers invaded the region in the 1800s and changed the course of the country forever.

One of the European powers, the British, clashed with the sultans of Zanzibar. The struggle was over control of a major source of manpower—the slave trade. The battle between the British and the sultans temporarily pushed the slave trade overland to Somalia's southern ports. Some of the slaves were used for agriculture. Today, the Bantu-Somalis descend from the forced labor of this period.

ROCK PAINTINGS AND OTHER FINDS

There are numerous archaeological sites in Somalia, but few have been thoroughly explored. In the north, burial sites containing bones, Stone Age weapons, and domestic items have been unearthed. Rock paintings and Stone Age artifacts have also been uncovered along the northern coast.

Many of the rock paintings depict animals such as giraffes, domesticated canines, and wild antelopes. Beneath each rock painting is an inscription, but archaeologists have not yet deciphered the meanings of this form of ancient writing.

Many of them believe that the rock paintings are over 2,500 years old. More rock etchings were discovered in 2005 at Laas Ga'al, outside Hargeysa, the capital of the self-declared Republic of Somaliland. The paintings are vivid, with stark outlines depicting early settlers worshipping large lyre-shaped or arch-horned cattle. Some regard Laas Ga'al to be the most significant rock painting site in all of Africa.

In Las Anod (Laasaanood), located in the region of Sool, under the control of the Republic of Somaliland, expeditions have located the remains of another city. More than 200 buildings, recognized as being built in the same style as the older part of Mogadishu, were found within this city. This perhaps indicates that the same types of people lived in Mogadishu and in Las Anod. Mogadishu itself contains an old city dating back to the 13th century, called Hammawein, which includes a central market and a mosque.

Even though these rich finds have been discovered, most archaeological sites in Somalia remain largely unprotected. Civil unrest combined with the population explosion and high unemployment has made the looting of historically and culturally significant sites a profitable business activity.

FOREIGN INTEREST IN SOMALIA

The battle for control over Somalia in the 19th century involved Great Britain and Italy, with Egypt and Ethiopia also wanting a stake. In 1839 the British annexed Aden, a city across the Red Sea on the Arabian Peninsula, and entered into two treaties with Somali sultanates to supply cattle to Somalia.

By 1869 the Egyptians (victorious after declaring their independence from the waning Ottoman Empire) were keen to expand their domain. The Egyptians managed to establish a skeleton administration in Berbera and Zeila for about one decade. In 1884 the British drove the Egyptians from Somalia, signed treaties with the Somali clans, and set up a protectorate along the coast. Meanwhile, Italy was concentrating on Somalia's Indian Ocean coast and its southern area.

In 1891 and 1894 two treaties were signed by Britain and Italy, specifying the boundaries of their influence in the region. Somalis were excluded from these negotiations and had no say on the matter. Italy also defined its boundaries with Ethiopia in 1897. A third European presence, the French, was also pulled into this political equation by the British who wanted their presence there in the early 1880s. The French established a colony in the north of Somalia by the middle of the 19th century.

This unwelcomed European control became an increasing source of discontent and resentment among the local Somalis. A Muslim leader, Mohammed bin Abdullah, appealed to the people to join him in a jihad, or holy war, against the European Christians. He began his campaign by forming an army in the northern coastal town of Berbera.

Mohammed bin Abdullah was highly respected, even venerated, by his disciples, but the European Christians dismissed him as a fanatic. The European settlers later discovered, to their high cost, that they had greatly underestimated him. The "Mad Mullah," as he came to be known, fought and killed thousands of Europeans.

In 1910 the British withdrew from the Somali interior. During World War I, the Germans and Turks supported Mohammed in his fight against the British. But in 1920 the British bombed Mohammed's camp, forcing him to flee. Mohammed died a natural death later that year.

Two British officers of the early 19th century purchasing sheep and goats from the Somalis.

COLONIAL POWERS AT WAR

In 1936 Italy invaded Ethiopia from Italian Somaliland. Three years later, when World War II broke out in Europe, the two colonial powers in Somalia, Britain and Italy, were on opposite sides. The two countries concentrated on their war efforts in Europe, but they also fought each other in Somalia.

The British formed battalion units in the Somali regions under their control, and the Italians organized themselves in the south. In August 1940 the Italians invaded and captured British Somaliland. But the British, swift to retaliate, managed both to reclaim their protectorate and to capture the Italian territories in 1941.

The British then sent military administrators to govern their extensive colonies in the Somali peninsula. They moved their capital from Berbera to Hargeysa and started a more developmental approach to governance during and shortly after World War II. The British opened nonreligious or secular schools, reorganized the court system, improved agricultural workers' working conditions, and created district and provincial councils. The British retained control in Italian Somaliland but had to contend with the rise of Somali nationalism and an indigenous political organization in the region, the Somali Youth League (SYL).

ROAD TO INDEPENDENCE

After World War II had ended, the Allied powers allowed Italy to regain its sphere of control in Somalia. But a major condition was attached—Italy had to help Somalia become independent by 1960. Youth groups, such as SYL and HDMC, were to play important roles in preparing Somalia for independence.

ITALIAN SOMALILAND The Somali Youth League (SYL) was the most successful political group out of those that contested the 1954 municipal elections held there. It obtained 48 percent of the vote. The HDMS received 22 percent, and 20 other parties took 30 percent of the vote.

In the general election of 1956, the SYL once again received a staggering victory with the most votes. Many existing parties ended up joining the SYL instead. In 1959 the SYL resorted to drastic measures in order to gain full control before independence in the following year. It arrested hundreds of members from rival groups and shut down many of their headquarters. Consequently, the party won 83 out of 90 seats in the 1959 elections. The SYL then attempted to balance the conflicting interests of its clan members, which was a problem area both within and outside the party.

BRITISH SOMALILAND Unlike the Italians, the British prohibited Somalis from forming political parties until they had obtained independence. The first British Somaliland election was held in 1959, but the Somaliland National League (SNL) refused to take part, convinced that the British would rig the election. The SNL participated in the second election held in February 1960, and won 20 out of 33 legislative seats. The Somali Youth League did not win a single seat in this election. In a surprise move in April 1960, Britain decided that it would grant independence to its British colony a few days after Italian Somaliland had become independent. This led Somali leaders from both territories to meet and to unify the two territories as one nation before the momentous occasion in July.

EARLY POLITICAL GROUPS

The Somali Youth Club (SYC), the first modern Somali political organization, started in 1943 as a reaction against modern-day European colonization. Its first members were 13 Somalis from a wide range of backgrounds. Many Somali police officers that the British had trained also joined the SYC. The British, who believed it would help combat the growing Italian influence, encouraged this. By 1946 over 25,000 Somalis belonged to the SYC, and the organization spread from Mogadishu to British Somaliland, Ethiopia, and Kenya.

A year later the group changed its name to the Somali Youth League (SYL) and focused on unifying Somali territories and protecting Somali interests. It also aimed at developing a modern educational system and a written Somali language. Moreover, the SYL worked toward the growth of a strong national identity and the elimination of clan divisions.

The SYL acted as a spur to others to form political groups. The Patriotic Benefit Union, later called the Hizbia Digil-Mirifle Somali (HDMS), emerged during the late 1940s. The HDMS had its base in the fertile agricultural region between the Jubba and Shabelle rivers. It regarded the British-influenced SYL as a rival party and consequently accepted help from the Italians, including cash donations.

FREE BUT RIPE FOR REVOLUTION

As planned, the British and Italians loosed their hold on Somalia in July 1960. The northern and southern regions finally united and formed the independent nation of Somalia.

Although the Somali people were joyful to be finally rid of the colonial yoke, other obstacles to true independence lay ahead. The country's new leaders were faced with the formidable task of unifying the peoples of two territories who spoke similar dialects, yet held different political views and administrative systems. They also operated different educational systems, and had separate currencies.

To assist in the task of unification, the United Nations appointed a Commission for Integration to merge the laws and cultures of the two regions. But tension between the clans of the north and south continued, leading to warfare and political revolutions. Within a few years of its independence, Somalia was to experience the breakdown of its democratically elected government and come under Communist rule. Also, from 1991 to late 2006, it slid into anarchy due to the absence of a strong central government.

THE GREAT SOMALI FAMINE

A devastating drought between 1974 and 1981 caused a great famine in Somalia. The world saw pictures of animal carcasses strewn over the desert sands, worsened by lingering images of people starving to death. Charities and aid organizations such as Save the Children Fund, International Christian Relief, and Action Aid sent relief workers to help.

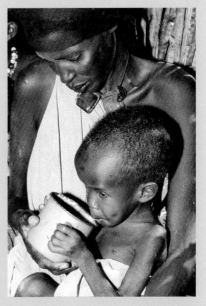

Somalis from all over the country walked for miles to arrive at the refugee camps. Extra food was given to emaciated children, pregnant women, nursing mothers, the elderly, and the sick. Everyone else received small rations of food twice a day. Medication, tents, toilets, vehicles and educational materials were also supplied. The disastrous drought finally ended in 1981 when the rains came. But these brought a new crisis in the form of flash floods. The parched ground could not absorb the rainfall, and there was no vegetation left from the drought to stop the rush of water over the land.

In the 1990s rural Somalis were hit by another severe famine. Although the international volunteers were there again to distribute food, many Somalis had to jostle for handouts. Some, who did not want to depend on the refugee camps, wandered around the countryside in search of food for their families and livestock. Many died as a result. Due to the worldwide publicity given to various famines, many still think of Somalia as a parched land without food.

GOVERNMENT

THE NEW GOVERNMENT OF 1960 drafted and adopted a constitution that sought to unify the two regions formerly controlled by Italy and Britain. Mogadishu was chosen as the new capital—a move that angered the northern Somalis, who did not want a southern town to be the capital.

The new government, however, went through numerous internal conflicts that, coupled with a weak economy, allowed for the success of a military coup by Major General Mohammed Siad Barre. Opposition fronts and militias based on different clans finally ousted Barre from power in 1991.

From then on Somalia slid into chaos, and internal warfare spiraled out of control. Although the Transitional National Government (TNG) was established in 2000 to reconcile the warring factions, the government held no real power outside its small base in Mogadishu. After the mandate of the TNG expired in 2003, the subsequent Transition Federal Government (TFG), based in Baidoa, was formed in 2004.

COUP OF OCTOBER 1969

In 1967 Somalia's interim president, Abdi Rashid Ali Shermarke, the former prime minister of its first government, was shot and killed by one of his bodyguards—apparently for political reasons.

At the same time, a coup was being planned by the army, which was discontented with the civilian government. Their disappointed hopes were echoed by the Somali people in general.

On October 21, 1969, southern armies captured Mogadishu and abducted government leaders. Major General Mohammed Siad Barre was the leader of this combined army maneuver and police coup. He deployed a tank outside Prime Minister Mohammed Egal's house and assumed control of the country, proclaiming himself head of state.

Opposite: **Monument of a military plane, found in the city center of Hargeysa.**

Mohammed Siad Barre, who took control of Somalia in a coup and proceeded to rule it with an iron hand.

Western powers suspected the Soviet Union to be behind the coup, because Siad Barre and his fellow revolutionaries immediately established a Communist government.

Siad Barre was tough and ruthless. He threw out the Somali constitution, banned all political parties, and abolished the National Assembly. His government openly toed the Soviet line and began to disseminate Communist propaganda on street corners. Every home was required to display a portrait or photograph of President Siad Barre.

Even artists and poets were forced to incorporate Communist propaganda into their works. His nepotistic and ironhanded rule resulted in an insurgence of strife and discontent.

SEVERING OF SOVIET TIES

Somalia, with Communism as the central form of government, was seen as a "Soviet satellite" by the West. Siad Barre remained firmly in power, surviving all attempts to oust him. In a sudden turn of events, however, Siad Barre's friendship with the Soviets was severely strained during the 1970s.

As part of his attempt to win disputed territory from Ethiopia, he encouraged a military group called the Western Somali Liberation Front (WSLF) to attack Ethiopian troops along the border. The resulting conflict became known as the Ogaden War.

Somewhat surprisingly, the Soviet Union supported Ethiopia rather than its "satellite," Somalia, in this war. This so enraged Siad Barre that he expelled all Soviet advisers from the country. The Ogaden War continued until 1978. The impact was widespread, causing civilian suffering and a dismal economic state for Somalia.

Siad Barre was finally forced to seek help from other countries. Eventually the United States, Britain, Egypt, Italy, and Saudi Arabia came to his aid, but on condition that he was not to turn to the Soviets again.

DOWNFALL OF SIAD BARRE

In 1979, on the tenth anniversary of his military coup, Siad Barre announced that Somalia was to be a socialist state. His brand of socialism, Scientific Socialism, was a loose combination of Islamic principles with influences from Marx, Lenin, Mao, and Mussolini.

Yet the country fared no better over the next decade. Droughts and civil wars took their toll, even with the foreign aid that came in. The northern Somali clans, bitterly opposed to southern leadership, waited for an opportunity to revolt. With the country in a state of war and the people on the brink of mass starvation, Siad Barre fled the country in 1991 and went into exile in Nigeria.

In 1992 the UN interceded to offer humanitarian relief by providing food supplies to the starving Somalis. But warlords looted UN relief planes upon landing and hijacked the food convoys. Thus, the operation was thwarted. Also, aid workers were assaulted. The UN appealed to the United States for help, and it responded by sending U.S. troops that same year to crack down on the looting and extortion that had prevented food aids from reaching the suffering civilians. Their combined effort was called Operation Restore Hope. The UN soon expanded its mission by trying to help Somalia establish political stability as well as maintain law and order.

Propaganda posters of the 1970s outside a government office served to remind the nation of who was still firmly in power.

*When Siad Barre
fled in early
1991, he left the
country in a
state of anarchy.
Civil war raged,
thus crippling
the economy.
All foreign aids
had been cut off
because of the end
of the cold war
and Somalia's
poor human rights
record.*

Nevertheless, events took a turn for the worse when an incident occurred involving 24 Pakistani soldiers being ambushed and massacred during an inspection of Somali arms weapons storage. U.S. troops were again mobilized, and they came in 1993 to help to capture those believed to be responsible. The mission proved to be largely unsuccessful.

The presence of U.S. forces led to several events that made international headlines. News pictures, for instance, showed Somali troops driving through the streets of Mogadishu, dragging the body of a U.S. soldier behind their vehicle. Heavy firefighting in late October left 18 U.S troops dead and about 90 injured. Escalating violence resulted in the U.S. military withdrawing from Somalia in March 1994. The UN followed soon after, in 1995, leaving Somalia without any official government to take over.

TRANSITIONAL ADMINISTRATIONS

Currently, in early 2007, Somalia has no permanent national government. A transitional government was created in 2000, but its authority was recognized only by the international community and not by Somaliland, Puntland, and the various warlords in the south.

In fact, warlords from southwest Somalia had declared autonomy for six districts in the region to form the Southwestern Regional Government. On the other hand, Jubaland, which had declared its independence from Somalia in 1998, supported the formation of the transitional government.

In 2004 a two-year peace process initiated by the government of Kenya, with the backing of the Intergovernmental Authority on Development (IGAD), along with the support of the African Union (AU), the European Union (EU), the UN, and the United States, bore some results.

The Transitional Federal Government (TFG) was established in November 2004 and based in Baidoa. It has an executive branch of government, which is currently headed by Abdullahi Yusuf Ahmed, who was elected as Transitional Federal President of Somalia. The interim prime minister selected by him is Ali Mohamed Ghedi.

In addition, the new interim governing body is called the Somalia Transitional Federal Institutions (Somalia TFI). It includes a 275-member parliamentary body, the Transitional Federal Assembly (TFA), a 31-member cabinet appointed by the prime minister and approved by the TFA. The Transitional Federal Government (TFG) has only the executive and legislative branches formed; the judiciary branch is still being developed.

UNION OF ISLAMIC COURTS

Although all Somali clan groups and leaders had participated in the formation of the TFG, a group challenged the interim government.

In 2004 in a bid to restore order in Mogadishu through the enforcement of Islamic law, a group that called itself the Union of Islamic Courts (UIC), contested the TFG, which had not been able to establish itself in Mogadishu. This network consisted of clerics and militiamen. Their rise

Abdullahi Yusuf Ahmed has been Somalia's interim president since 2004. He was elected by 189 out of 275 Somali members of parliament. He is a former warlord and ex-president of Puntland.

THE LEGISLATURE AND JUDICIARY

The Transitional Federal Assembly (TFA) is a unicameral National Assembly with 275 members. Sixty-one seats are reserved for each of Somalia's four major clans, the Darod, Digil-Mirifle, Dir, and Hawiye. The rest of the 31 seats are divided among minority clans.

Somalia has no national legal system, but is in the process of rebuilding this. However, the TFG's reach is still limited. Disputes are resolved either through traditional (tribal) Somali law or Sharia (Islamic) law.

to power saw the UIC seizing control of Mogadishu and much of the south from warlords during the months of June and July 2006. Some Somalis looked on the UIC as relief after 15 years of terror by various warlords that destabilized Somalia. UIC is completely tribally anchored and promotes Islamic law. Ten of UIC's eleven courts are associated with the Hawiye clan. Although the Hawiye is divided into subclans, each UIC court must still prosecute members of their own subclan in order to elude accusations of clan bias.

The UIC's dominance in Mogadishu made life for the people more bearable. UIC's powerful militia and fighting gunmen became Somalia's formidable armed forces. Extortions from warlords ceased, and Mogadishu's airports and seaports were reopened for the first time since 1995. UIC also validated transactions such as house purchases and oversaw weddings and divorces. The UIC's influence had increased to such a level that peace talks were proposed with the interim government to come to some concession and eventually form a unified national army. In September 2006 neither the transitional government nor the UIC turned up for the scheduled meeting for talks, so the talks failed to occur.

Matters took a turn for the worse in December when UIC assaulted the interim government's stronghold in Baidoa, which was guarded by the latter's military. As these troops were backed by Ethiopia, UIC also declared war with Ethiopia for its intervention in Somali affairs. Ethiopian forces soon joined the fray on December 24, armed with aircraft, tanks, and artillery support for the interim government. After two weeks of intense fighting, the UIC was overpowered. Their six-month occupation of southern Somalia ended. They soon abandoned the capital and their last stronghold, the port town of Kismaayo, south of Mogadishu.

Somalis are still divided, and those who supported the UIC have lingering doubts and maintain some distrust for TFG and vice versa. The renewal of fighting has opened the country to fears that it would return to its former lawless state, as warlords will probably jostle for control. There are also fears that the UIC would now engage in an insurgency. Currently, the government has called on international humanitarian aid and also the African Union (AU) to help stabilize the country.

CRIME AND HUMAN RIGHTS ABUSES

The collapse of Somalia's state and economy has also seen deterioration of human rights for the civilian population. Killings, kidnappings, rape, and other atrocities were inflicted daily on ordinary Somalis in the warfare between north and south. Insecurity in the south has also made it difficult for foreign peacekeeping forces to offer assistance. To escape factional fighting, more than a million Somalis from the south fled to the north of Somalia and to neighboring countries such as Yemen, Kenya, Djibouti, Ethiopia, and Burundi. Some fled even as far as Sri Lanka. Escape is only marginally better, as many of these internally displaced people suffered from poor refugee camp conditions and were often subjected to rape, kidnapping, and looting by armed groups. Arbitrary arrests, allegations of torture, and detention without trial are also often reported. Courts in Puntland and Somaliland frequently do not practice fair trials.

In December 2004 a 16-year-old child was convicted of espionage and was imprisoned for five years. She was unfairly tried and her rights as a child were not recognized. Journalists were also arrested, and some were even beaten for reporting on human rights abuses or for criticizing political authorities.

Besides the Republic of Somaliland that declared independence in 1991, the self-proclaimed autonomous state of Puntland has been self-governing since 1998.

ECONOMY

SOMALIA'S STATUS REMAINS that of a Third World country. In the years since independence in 1960, the economy has picked up only slightly. The economy continues to be dependent largely on agriculture and animal herding.

The public sector played a dominant role when Siad Barre implemented his socialist policies and abolished private ownership of banks, insurance companies, and wholesale trade. By 1989 there were rampant inflation and soaring food prices. Wages in the towns and cities stagnated. By 1992, after the collapse of the socialist government, Western powers were again supplying aid to the country, and the economy of several cities improved. Continual civil strife and the collapse of central authority, however, have greatly weakened Somalia's already struggling economy.

Somalia's untapped natural resources have also made it vulnerable to world market vagaries and too dependent on remittances from abroad. Irregular rainfall and periodic bans on the import of livestock have also

Left: **A bustling scene, as these settled nomads collect the corn harvest in sacks for sale to the wholesale traders.**

Opposite: **A Somali trader selling her wares at a market.**

severely impaired its economy. It is in the face of these many formidable challenges that Somalia's Transitional Federal Government (TFG) must try to rebuild the country's economy.

AGRICULTURE AND LIVESTOCK

When there are good harvests, cotton, sesame, groundnuts, sugarcane, corn, and sorghum are exported. In the water-scarce Woqooyi Galbeed region in the northwest, most Somali farmers are agropastoralist. They engage mostly in crop cultivation on drylands,

Somali children prepare the ground for planting corn in the next season.

growing crops such as corn and millet, as these plants do not need much water. In the south, near the Jubba and Shabelle rivers, wet farming is practiced, and sugarcane, bananas, cotton, and rice are grown.

Although agricultural production today is not on par with prewar levels, the Northwest Integrated Agricultural Development Project and several other international and local nongovernmental organizations (NGOs) have helped to provide technical and financial assistance to farming communities. Livestock accounts for 65 percent of Somalia's export earnings. Much of the country's livestock is exported to Egypt and Saudi Arabia.

In 2000 Somalia's livestock industry suffered a setback when Saudi Arabia and other Persian Gulf states banned exports of Somali livestock due to an outbreak of Rift Valley fever. This hemorrhagic disease is caused by mosquitoes that hatch from virus-infected eggs bred in contaminated floodwater. The outbreak claimed the lives of 80 Somalis, mostly living in the south.

The ban is still in effect although the disease has not been detected in Somalia in recent years.

FISHERIES

Many types of fish live on the rocky sea bottom along the seemingly endless stretch of Somali coast.

The most common are anchovy, sardine, tuna, herring, and mackerel. Other plentiful varieties of seafood are flounder, snapper, shark, spiny lobster, oyster, octopus, and clam.

Somalis on the whole are not great fish eaters even with the richness of their coastal waters. Because of this, the country did not seriously engage in commercial fishing until the 1970s. Fishing cooperatives were created in 1974 to purchase boats and fishing gear and to look after the handling and marketing aspects. Cooperatives in the big coastal cities were encouraged to go retail and sell most of their fresh fish directly to the public.

In spite of such measures, only 1 percent of Somalis are fishermen. With its small fishing fleet; lack of industrial operators, refrigerated storage, processing, and transportation infrastructure; piracy off its southern coastline; and unregulated fishing, Somalia's fishing industry is not inclined to improve.

The December 2004 tsunami also resulted in severe damage to its northeastern ports, adding to Somalia's woes.

Fish are plentiful along the Somali coast, but it was only in the 1970s that commercial fishing began to be taken seriously.

INDUSTRIAL GROWTH

There has been some industrial growth in Somalia over the past few decades. Foreign interests have set up fisheries, tanneries, pharmaceutical plants, sugar refineries, and petroleum and uranium mining facilities.

With the help of the Soviets in the 1970s, the government built five large plants for meat, dairy, and fish processing. By the late 1970s,

As of October 2006, 1,473 Somali shillings (SOS) are equivalent to one U.S dollar.

the state owned 53 large and modern manufacturing plants. Most of these industries now lie in wretched ruins. Rampant looting during the civil war stripped most warehouses, industrial facilities, and small businesses.

After World War II deposits of petroleum and natural gas were discovered in Somalia. Uranium, iron ore, and other minerals were discovered, too, but the commercial extraction of these natural resources was restricted until 1981. Today, because of the uncertain economic and political climate, these resources remain largely untapped.

In Mogadishu, light industry is thriving with about 25 processing plants. Some of the products manufactured include pasta, mineral water, packaging, textiles, leather, and refined sugar. In 2004 the Coca-Cola company boosted industry confidence when it opened a bottling plant in Mogadishu. Today, Mogadishu's largest market offers a range of goods from food to the latest electronic gadgets. The main port and airport have reopened after being closed for 15 years.

Although the country has no formal banking sector, it has several remittance services. Somalia's large diaspora community (Somalis living and working abroad) sends back to Somalia $500 million to $1 billion in remittance annually, making money exchange services a thriving industry in Somalia.

TRANSPORTATION

Somalia has poorly developed road systems. There are no railways connecting major cities and towns in spite of efforts made in the early 1970s, when hundreds of roads were built.

Today most of these roads have become run-down and neglected because of poor maintenance and a lack of funding. Somalia now has only 1,800 miles (2,897 km) of passable roads, and most of them are not accessible during the rainy seasons.

Somalia's deepwater ports also share the same poor condition, yet smaller ports located at Merca, Baraawe, and Boosaaso are still in use. The absence of security is still an issue at most Somali ports.

EMPLOYMENT AND TRADE

Current figures place Somalia's workforce at 3.7 million. Out of this, 71 percent are employed in agriculture and 29 percent have industry and service-related occupations. Farms produce bananas, sorghum, corn, coconuts, rice, sugarcane, and other crops. Animals such as cattle, sheep, goats, and fish are also reared.

Light industries consist of sugar refining, textiles, and wireless communications. Some 40 percent of the country's gross domestic product comes from livestock trading. The other export commodities are bananas, animal hides, charcoal, and scrap metal.

Economic life in the cities tends to be relaxed and casual. Businessmen spend almost as much time at the coffeehouse as in the office, regarding the coffee shop as a place to meet, discuss politics, conduct business transactions, and keep in touch with contacts.

The driver of this old truck stuck on a beach is fortunate to have willing helpers. The lack of a decent road system in many parts of Somalia means drivers must use whatever ways they can in getting from one spot to another.

Somalis favor four-wheel drive vehicles and motorcycles for road driving. In the cities they also travel by bus, taxi, and private car. But many town and city dwellers still travel by foot or in a donkey cart. Even in the largest cities people walk down the streets with their goats, camels, and cattle.

Air transportation is provided by small air charter firms and private airlines like Air Somalia and Daallo Airlines. The capital, Mogadishu,

has an international airport, and other cities such as Hargeysa have small domestic airports. Currently Somalia has an estimated 15 airlines and 60 aircrafts that ply six international destinations and several domestic routes.

THE MEDIA AND TELECOMMUNICATIONS

Although Somalia is about the same size as Texas, in the past it had only three radio stations and one television station.

Until the overthrow of Siad Barre, the government controlled radio and television programming. Political propaganda messages were frequently broadcast instead. Today there are numerous media sources, including nine radio and four television stations.

The print media in Somalia are primarily in Somali, Arabic, and English. The socialist government used to control and censor their contents. Today, most of the newspapers promote membership in a particular clan or political group. Unfortunately, financial and technical constraints restrict many Somalis' access to television or print media.

Newspapers and radio tend to have mostly local and regional audiences, rather than national ones. To Somalis, radio is an important mass medium. Like the newspapers, radio in Somalia tends to have clan biases. The Somalis obtain international news largely through television from the Cable News Network (CNN) and the British Broadcasting Corporation's (BBC) daily radio program.

Somalia also has three Internet service providers (ISPs)—Telcom, Nationlink, and Hormuud—all vying for some 90,000 Internet users. The booming telecommunications industry has not only seen the increase of phone companies but also mobile phone users. As of 2005, about 500,000 Somalis were recorded as cell phone users.

ENVIRONMENT

SOMALIA IS DOMINATED by highlands and rugged mountains in the north, with low plains and valleys in the south. This varied landscape is host to an abundantly diverse variety of plants and animals.

The collapse of Somalia's central government during the civil war and the prevailing absence of a strong government have set off a deplorable and catastrophic chain of events for its environment. Lawlessness and the greedy pursuit of personal gain have resulted in human activities that have damaged Somalia's fragile ecosystem. Its environmental problems range from deforestation to the indiscriminate poaching of wildlife.

Somalis, in general, also do not support the idea of sustainable development—the renewal of natural resources.

The country's uncertain political climate and lack of financial resources have made the implementation of measures to tackle its host of environmental issues difficult.

Relative peace was enjoyed during the short period when the Union of Islamic Courts (UIC) rose and controlled Somalia from mid-2006 to the very begining of 2007.

Now long-term political stability is again hanging in the balance. Any future hopes for the environment will depend on the realization of a strong, stable central government and enforcement of legislature to protect and conserve the Somali natural landscape and wildlife.

LAND DEGRADATION

Somalia's landscape is set against a backdrop of sparse savanna interspersed with a few forested areas. Roughly 29,016 square miles (75,150 square km), or 12 percent of the land's total area, is covered with forests. Somalis are highly dependent on their land. Nomads, who make up about 60 percent of the population, and their animal herds rely upon the land

Opposite: **Somali children enjoy playing in waters off the coast of Mogadishu.**

for pasture and shelter. The rest of the residents exploits the land for crop cultivation. As a result of this extensive, unsustainable use of the land, grave environmental problems such as deforestation, overgrazing, and soil erosion are inevitable.

DEFORESTATION A large number of Somalis are heavily reliant on trees and their by-products for shelter, fuel, and income.

Nomads from the middle and northern regions build their makeshift homes from timber cut from trees as they roam the land in search of water and pasture. Camels, sheep, and cattle are herded mainly in the middle and northern zones, as well as parts of the eastern sectors such as Mudug and Sanaag. These animals make up most of the livestock that grazes in these regions, thus exacerbating another environmental problem: overgrazing and soil erosion. In the area between Mogadishu and Kismaayo, for example, overgrazing has resulted in desertification, causing the coastal sand dunes to gradually move inland.

The population in the south, on the other hand, fell and clear trees for farming, land cultivation, and charcoal. One of the major charcoal industries in southern Somalia is located in Kismaayo, near the Jubba River.

Trees are the primary source of fuels such as charcoal and firewood. But trees in Somalia are felled faster than they are reforested. More than 80 percent of the dominant tree species, the *Acacia busei*, is cut down for both local and foreign consumption.

Somalia has a total forest area of 17.54 million acres (7.1 million ha). Between 1990 and 2005 it lost 13.9 percent of its forest cover, an estimated 2.4 million acres (0.99 million ha). The rate of deforestation keeps increasing. Between 2000 and 2005 the rate accelerated by

10.4 percent. Somalia thus loses about 1.02 percent of its forests annually.

Somalia's limited wooded forests and the pressure made by local demands for fuel are further compounded by the need to export charcoal in return for essential foreign currency. In rural Somalia, charcoal making provides employment for many. Lured by quick returns on investments, warlords and local businessmen have invested in battery-powered chain saws to cut down the greatest number of trees in the shortest time possible. These trees are then burned and made into charcoal. Trucks carry the charcoal to ports in Mogadishu, Kismaayo, and Boosaaso for export. It is estimated that 30,000 tons of charcoal are exported every month, mostly to Gulf countries.

Aside from charcoal, trees are also made into wooden furniture and boats. Certain species of trees native to Somalia, such as the frankincense and myrrh trees, are highly prized for their commercial value. Their secretions are processed into aromatic resins valued by many.

DESERTIFICATION Deforestation and overgrazing retard soil formation. Trees and shrubs are crucial in controlling water runoff and protecting topsoil from the fierce Somali dust storms, especially over the eastern plains. Desertification occurs when trees and shrubs do not act as covers, exposing the soil to the elements. The soil then becomes barren and unable to host vegetation or livestock for many years.

A frankincense tree oozing the important and fabled resin.

Volunteers planting vegetation in hope of slowing down desertification.

Desertification is already evident along the Somali coast where mangrove trees are felled for timber and in the overgrazed Sanaag plateau in northern Somalia.

The charcoal industry is one of the main culprits responsible for abusing Somali land to the point that it no longer can support much plant life. To provide wood and charcoal to satisfy regional needs as well as international demand, bushes and other small plants are sacrificed for the burning of larger trees. As a result, land suitable for grazing is destroyed. Furthermore, trucks that carry the charcoal for export leave in their wake deep land tracks that are transformed into gullies after the rains. If deforestation is left unchecked much longer, it could severely affect Somalis' livelihoods. In the long run, nomads' traditional lifestyle may be threatened because of the lack of pasture for their livestock. For rural Somalis, it would become increasingly difficult to cultivate crops when the land becomes less fertile.

It is difficult, in the present political climate, to investigate and put a stop to deforestation. The lack of a strong central government has created opportunities for rival warlords and profit-driven businessmen to exploit the land for their own gain without regard for the natural environment. It is thus unsurprising that the areas with the worst rates of deforestation are in the south, where the warlords reign. Middle and Lower Jubba and Middle and Lower Shabelle are hit particularly hard.

ENDANGERED ANIMALS

The civil war's lasting 15 years, exacerbated by widespread poaching and deforestation, have taken a heavy toll on Somalia's wildlife. At last count there were about 642 species of birds, 222 mammals, 182 reptiles, and 32 amphibians living in Somalia. Out of those, 18 of the country's mammalian and 8 bird species were threatened with extinction.

In 1980 there were about 400,000 elephants, but because they were hunted extensively for their ivory, they are almost gone today. The number of lions has also shrunk to between 500 and 750. Other endangered species include the black rhinoceros, Pelzeln's dorcas gazelle, the African wild ass, the hawksbill turtle, the green turtle, and the humphead wrasse (one of the largest coral reef fishes in the world).

SOMALI GOLDEN MOLE

Habitat degradation such as deforestation and soil erosion caused the Somali golden mole to be considered a critically endangered species between 1996 and 2004. The mole was taken off the endangered species list in 2006, however, and was reclassified as "data deficient" due to insufficient sampling. While the existence of this blind, subterranean mammal was documented some 250 years ago, current knowledge about this little animal of the *genus Chlorotalpa* still remains limited.

What is known about this creature is that it can be found in the dense bush and savannas of southern Somalia where the soil is loose and sandy. The golden mole's shiny coat of dense fur varies from black to pale tawny yellow but has an iridescent sheen. It breeds throughout the year, peaking perhaps during the wetter months when there is abundant prey. Its litter size is small, with about one or two young per birth. It weighs between 1.4 to 2.7 ounces (40 to 75 g), and has no visible eyes or ears. Its diet consists of earthworms, snails, and insects like crickets, grasshoppers, and locusts.

A male lion resting in the shade yet ever vigilant, watchful of intruders and incoming danger to its pride.

CONSERVATION EFFORTS

The leading environmental organization in Somalia is the Environmental Protection and Anti-Desertification Organization (SEPADO), which was established in 1996. Even with a short supply of funds, SEPADO has helped improve environmental awareness in the country. In its bid to tackle the country's environmental problems, SEPADO distributed educational flyers and stickers to the populace and gave advice and training to farmers on sustainable agricultural practices. Other plans in the pipeline include the creation of tree nurseries and reforestation programs.

SEPADO is also canvassing for funds and partnerships from international bodies to help more Somalis to conserve their environment. To tackle problems caused by the charcoal industry, SEPADO has also appealed to the Federal Environmental Agency of the United Arab Emirates to ban charcoal exports from Somalia.

Furthermore, Somalia has three national parks, located at Kismaayo, Hargeysa, and Mogadishu. It also has about 14 protected areas. But as there are no national environmental policies in place, these parks and reserves are largely neglected, and the scant rules that protect wildlife are poorly enforced. Somalia's interim government is currently looking at options to promote ecotourism as one of the ways to promote conservation and preservation of its wildlife.

In January 2006 an international conference on lion conservation was held in Johannesburg, South Africa. It was suggested that foreign trophy hunters be allowed to bag some of Somalia's lions. This will not only introduce controlled hunting to the country but also give it a much needed source of tourism revenue.

COASTLINE WORRIES

Seabirds, whales, sharks, dolphins, and turtles are among the abundant marine life in Somalia's waters. The richness of its seas indicates that the country's 2,422 miles (3,898 km) of coastline is well suited for ecotourism. Nonetheless, as its coastline and waters are uncared for and unprotected, because of the absence of effective governance and rampant piracy, this potential source of income is not being realized.

WASTE DUMPING In the 1990s Somali warlords and businessmen negotiated deals with industrialized nations to dump hazardous nuclear and chemical waste into the central eastern coast off Somalia for large amounts of money. It was reported that some of the alleged perpetrators were Swiss and Italian firms. Somalia's tenuous political situation, geographical accessibility, low public awareness, and poor economy have allowed its waters to be exploited and become a toxic dumping spot.

At the moment no extensive research has been done in Somalia to determine the environmental and human impact of waste dumping, but there have been a few worrying incidents. In the southwestern town of Bardheere, for example, it was reported that 120 people died after suffering nose bleeds. There also have been numerous reports that Somalis who were living near the coastline were dying after swallowing water from the sea. Recently, a study has associated the increase in the numbers of livestock death and human patients with cancer to the dumping of toxic waste in the country.

OIL SPILLS Adding to Somalia's environmental woes are oil and chemical spills caused by leaking tankers as they pass through the Arabian Sea. Somalia is unable to deal with these spills and has no contingency plans, even though it has the second-longest coastal area in all of Africa. The problem is now so bad that it is common to see tons of dead marine animals decaying beside the long seashore.

ILLEGAL FISHING Somali militias have entered into illegal fishing licensing arrangements with foreign countries. These underhanded agreements allow interested parties to fish in Somali waters using large sea-sweeping nets. These fishing methods not only exhaust Somalia's fishery resources but also endanger its economic sustainability. Moreover, these trawlers often net endangered by-catches such as turtles, dolphins, and manatees and also destroy critical reef habitats. Although the Somali Ministry of Fisheries issues licenses for those interested in conducting legal fishing in Somali seas, illegal fishing has continued to flourish for more than a decade.

Somalia is party to the Nairobi and Jeddah Regional Seas Conventions and the UN Convention on the Law of the Sea, which includes regulations on dealing with the pollution of the marine environment. Somalia is in no condition, however, to provide responsible marine governance. Although there are plans to promote marine ecotourism, eradicating illegal dumping and indiscriminate fishing may prove to be very challenging.

PREWAR ENVIRONMENTAL AGENCIES

Even before the collapse of the government in 1991, Somalia had no central governmental body for environmental protection and conservation, although there were several ministries and state agencies in charge of managing the natural environment.

The National Parks Agency, for example, was set up in 1970 to establish nationally protected areas and parks. As late as 1991, however, there were no protected nature sanctuaries in Somalia. By 2003 the situation improved slightly with 0.8 percent of Somalia's land being placed under environmental protection. This figure is still well below the target of 10 percent. The result of this lack of progress can be seen in the rapid rate of deforestation. Lost in 2000 were 297 square miles (769 square km) of forest. Also threatened with extinction are 17 plant species.

Another environmental body, the National Range Agency, was responsible for securing grazing and drought reserves as well as preventing and controlling soil erosion on the ranges. Established in 1976, the agency implemented only limited measures, one of which was to prohibit the export of charcoal and firewood.

With the collapse of the central government in 1991, the exports resumed, posing another major assault on Somalia's dwindling forests.

In 1977 the Ministry of Fisheries and Marine Resources was formed to prevent pollution of the sea. The agency exerted very little control along the coastline and pollution of the waters was never prevented.

SOMALIS

NOMADIC SOMALIS BELIEVE that all Somalis originated from a common father called Samalle (or Ham), who was a son of the biblical Noah. All Somalis belong to one or another of the six clans, or tribes, in the country.

Over 85 percent of the inhabitants are ethnic Somali, while the remaining 15 percent have Bantu, Arab, or European bloodlines. Although it is difficult to keep track of population changes, because of the large number of nomads and refugees, it is estimated that there are about 8.9 million people living in Somalia. Due to poverty and civil strife, the average life expectancy of a Somali is only 48.5 years. Women, on average, live to 50.3 years, men to only 46.7 years. About 44.4 percent of the population reaches the age of 14, while 53 percent are between 15 and 64 years of age. The rest, about 2.6 percent, are aged 65 and above.

Above: **Nomadic women putting up an** *akal*, **a traditional home made of sticks and animal skins.**

Opposite: **Somali women react delightedly as they watch a play in Mogadishu, the capital city of Somalia.**

Somalis are a family-oriented people; they place great importance on their relatives, line of descent, and clan membership. Children learn early about their lineage and clan associations.

Somalia has been called a "nation of poets," as most Somalis share a great love of poetry. They also believe strongly in their traditional way of life. This, more than anything else, has enabled them to endure the difficult years of colonialism, tyranny, civil war, famine, and poverty.

SOMALI MINORITIES

According to recent statistics, 15 percent of the population include peoples who are of Bantu, Arab, or European descent. They can trace their roots back to ancestors who intermarried with ethnic Somalis over the centuries. Somalis of Bantu lineage can be found inhabiting farming villages in the south. A small number of Somalis of Italian descent are also found there, dating back to Somalia's colonial era, when the southern territory came under Italian control. Those with Arab ancestry are usually found in coastal cities such as Mogadishu. This is because Arab and Persian traders established their first trading posts along the coast in the seventh and 10th centuries.

These leather tanners are from minority groups who traditionally take up this kind of occupation.

Somali Bantus are the descendents of six African tribes in East Africa. Forced into slavery by Arab traders, the Bantus endured years of hardship in Somalia. Eventually the Bantus assimilated themselves into Somali society and established themselves as farmers.

Like other minorities who did not have armed militias, they suffered from the armed bullies of the fighting factions. During the civil war in the 1990s, their farms were raided, women were raped and men were killed. As a result, there was an exodus of Somali Bantus to neighboring Kenya and Tanzania for protection.

The few Bantus that remain in Somalia today have resumed their farming activities, yet warlord militias extort protection money in exchange for not harming them.

There are also other minorities in Somalia. Certain occupations such as hunting, metal working, and leather tanning are traditionally performed by Somalis from the so-called "lower castes." These people, who are indistinguishable from other Somalis and who speak the same language as their counterparts, have their own "clans," or occupational groups.

Some historians believe that members of these occupational clans are really Somalis by origin who had been ostracized from society because of the types of work they do. Many have lineages similar to those of existing Somali clans. But because these groups often speak a "secret" language (actually, nothing more than slang or occupational jargon), the pastoral and agricultural clans have regarded them as a people of unknown ethnic origins.

Even though Somali governments have tried to treat these minorities well and give them access to education and jobs, many common Somalis have continued to consider them as "lower caste." They make up less than 1 percent of the Somali population society.

Many of them, about three-quarters of the total, work as barbers, circumcisers, and hunters. They call themselves the Midgaan. Another group, the Tumaal, make up less than a quarter of the total, and are mostly metal craft workers. Notwithstanding their lowly status in Somali society, certain members of the occupational groups are consulted by middle- and upper-middle class Somalis, who believe them to have magical powers. They are hired on special occasions—to bless a Somali wedding, baptize a baby, or act as fortune tellers. Educated Somalis reject these prejudicial distinctions of the past.

These men from the same clan are aware of the importance of kinship for Somalis.

SOMALI SOCIAL SYSTEM

Somalia's social system centers around its clans. To function as a member of the Somali social system, a person must belong to a clan. Arabs and Persians who have migrated to Somalia often invent fictitious clan backgrounds to try to fit in, and foreign visitors often feel left out in this tight-knit society.

After colonial times, Somalis finally have a say in the future of their country. When it comes to choosing political sides and dealing with political confrontations, Somalis are obligated to remain loyal to his or her own personal family first. This is followed by the immediate lineage, then to the clan of lineage, and finally to the clan family.

A gunman protecting a harvest of corn in the town of Merca, in case of a raid by an opposing clan.

Kinship and extended families are important to the common people. Clan and clan family became important political tools since the opposition fronts that clashed with Siad Barre's regime. As time went by, the increase of clan-based influence grew. Siad Barre's regime and its divisive rule, compounded by the clan-based opposition movement, eventually led to the collapse of the state of Somalia.

This, coupled with clan-based violence and attempts at "ethnic cleansing" (genocide), gradually caused distrust and anger to develop. This culmination of mounting factors is probably the explanation of what underlies the division that exists in Somalia today.

The common people's support for the clan can also be motivated by political beliefs and affiliations. Thus, clan-based politics and violence are regarded as a political problem.

PRIDE IN CRAFTWORK

Since the time of the earliest settlers, Somalis have shown a talent for craftwork. They make sure the tools they use fit their hands well. To them, their tools are extensions of their hands, and they take pride in making and maintaining these tools.

An object, once crafted, may serve its owner for many years. This is especially true of the shepherd's stick, which the nomads carry with them wherever they go. A common Somali handicraft is the symbol of four triangles or a large triangle with four smaller triangles within it. The smaller triangles stand for the four corners of the world, and the large triangle symbolizes the eye of God. Other religious representations are the journey to Mecca and the life of the Prophet Muhammad.

Village craftsmen used to pass on their skills to their male children, but this tradition has eroded over the years as more Somalis move into towns and cities. Nevertheless, good examples of traditional Somali stonework, pottery, rugs, leatherwork, and jewelry can still be found in some villages.

This Somali craftsman uses an L-shaped tool for his work.

WAYS OF DRESSING

During the colonial period, rural nomadic men would usually wear a long white cloth that was wound around the waist and draped over the shoulders. Back then, many Somali men considered hair to be an important feature of their appearance. Some men would cover their heads with women's hair or with mud; others used henna to dye their hair or they would apply butter to their hair as an insect repellent.

Guntina (goon-TEE-nah), a long cloth in white or beautiful, colorful material, was traditionally worn by rural Somali women. It was wound around the body and fastened into a knot on the right shoulder. Married women held their hair back with a black scarf and wore another long flowing scarf over their head and arms.

A married Somali woman adorned with a head scarf and dressed in a bright red color.

In the modern setting today, most Somalis wear Western attire in public, at work, or in school. For leisure or in rural regions, many will revert to more traditional ways of dressing. Men wear a long white cloth or a *maccawiis*, a brightly colored cloth. Sometimes, they pair it with a Western shirt or shawl and accessorize with a *benadiry kufia*, a Somali cap.

Somali women generally wear full-length dresses in assorted styles. The *guntina* is still worn, either in simple white or red cotton, but the well-to-do often prefer more ostentatious designs. In north and northeastern Somali cities and rural areas, women are seen in thin cotton or polyester voile dresses over a full-length half slip and a brassiere. Married women adorn themselves with head scarves but are not veiled. But some women from conservative Arab families or fundamentalist backgrounds prefer to be veiled. Single girls braid their hair and do not apply make-up, perfume, or use incense for their hair. But urbanization has slowly eroded the distinction between married and unmarried women.

LIFESTYLE

THE NOMADS OF SOMALIA can be found roaming the land. In the past, their way of life was highly influenced by the ruthless Somali desert and climate changes. They would move families and herds over vast arid stretches of the countryside in search of pasture. Today, with modernization, some of the people use vehicles, like trucks, and have dug water holes and water sources. This nomadic lifestyle has basically remained unchanged for thousands of years.

Back in the 1970s and 1980s, severe droughts impacted the nomads as they and their animals were dying of thirst and starvation in the desert. Many were left with no other option than to seek help at refugee camps. As soon as the famines ended, nomads who survived left the camps for the scattered pasturelands once more.

Family and clan play highly important roles in the lives of the nomads. This is more so for the wandering nomads than for members of the seminomadic community. All nomads belong to one of four pastoral tribal clans. Because of the size of these clans, close associations among members are formed within each group, and subclans of between four to eight people are commonplace.

Members of these smaller groups are extremely supportive of one another. Traditionally, when one member of a subclan has a dispute with a member of another subclan, the two groups will attempt to mediate and settle the affair by exchanging camels. If the matter is not resolved, violence may erupt, with involved subclans mounting a vigorous defense.

Above: **Nomads load their donkey in preparation for the long trek ahead.**

Opposite: **A nomadic man traveling with his few possessions.**

Three generations of Somalis relaxing outside their house.

TRUE COUSINS

When Somalis refer to each other as brother or sister, the terms can include distant relatives, strangers, and actual siblings. Likewise, a Somali's "true cousin" can be someone two generations removed. Three generations separate second cousins, and third cousins are separated by four generations.

Although the Somali people trace their roots patrilineally, that is, through the father's side of the family, the mother plays a central role in Somali life.

Divorce is quite common in Somali society. A woman will frequently marry several men during her lifetime and bear children with each of them. Thus, children of different fathers remain with their mother after the fathers have left, remarried, or chosen to live with one of their other wives.

Child care is the woman's responsibility, and she usually will not want a former husband's new wife to look after her children. For this reason, a Somali child's closest ties are often forged with maternal relatives, in spite of the patrilineal nature of Somali society. Although, traditionally, a child is not obligated to maternal relatives, who do not bear ultimate responsibility for him or her, a child often consults or seeks assistance from these relatives when in need or in trouble.

HIERACHY OF LOYALTY

Somalis faithfully observe a chain of loyalty—family, lineage, subclan, clan or tribe, and nation. A popular saying in Somalia and in Arab nations summarizes this succinctly: "I against my brother; I and my brother against my cousin; I, my brother, and my cousin against the world." There is an exception to this rule. Because of the country's liberal views on divorce and bigamy, families tend to be very large. On average, a Somali woman gives birth to 6.76 children. That is why sometimes brothers and sisters with a common mother find themselves ranged on opposing sides, usually due to disagreements between their fathers. As their ultimate allegiance is toward their own father, bitter conflicts between half-siblings can result.

Somali children learn from a very young age to value an honorable reputation and to avoid harming the family or clan name. As Muslims, Somalis hold views on life that are greatly influenced by their religion. They believe, for instance, that fate controls their lives.

Most Somalis are convinced that men and women are not equal and are actually very different in both nature and social status. Somalis also hold the elderly in high regard, believing that wisdom increases with age.

This group of Somalis is related in various ways to each other.

SOMALIS' VIEW OF STRANGERS

Somalis are loyal and generous people who honor and support their family and friends. But they are cautious toward strangers, which sometimes offends foreigners. They are also wary of non-Muslims.

In general, however, after Somalis have made friends with a foreigner, they will become quite accommodating. Travelers who cannot find a place to stay may be invited into a Somali home for the night. On the other hand, not many foreign travelers visit the country. Due to its Communist past, civil wars, famines, and primitive amenities, Somalia is not a popular tourist spot. The Somalis are thus unaccustomed to foreigners, and it takes them a little while to warm up to strangers.

MARRIAGE AND POLYGAMY

Traditionally, Somali men decided whom they would marry and arranged all details with the father of the bride. This system of arranged marriages often led to older men paying a lot of money to the fathers of young girls in exchange for marriage agreements. Today younger Somalis tend to select a spouse based on typical marriage values such as love, honor, and respect.

Whether the marriage is arranged or not, the groom's family presents a gift of camels, cattle, or money to the bride's family. This gift is given serious consideration because it represents the esteem the groom-to-be has for his bride and her family. After the wedding, it is the bride's family who may have to present the young couple with a house. A marriage is not just a relationship between two people but also acts as a bridge between two separate families.

Most Somalis marry outside of their primary lineage, and the woman will leave her family or clan to live with her husband. Women, as a mark of loyalty to their own family, retain their family name upon marriage rather than assume their husband's last name.

During the marriage ceremony, which has to take place before a sheikh, a religious leader, the couple sign legal documents that stipulate how much money the man has to give his wife if they were to divorce. The settlement consists of money, animals, land, or jewelry, and immediately becomes the wife's personal property. Until a couple divorces, the husband keeps the property in trust. If it is the wife and not the husband who wants a divorce, the woman usually has to give up her right to this property.

Men driving their cattle home. A head of cattle is a welcome wedding gift for a bride's family.

Under Islamic law, polygamy is condoned—but for men only. A man may have as many as four wives at one time, if he can support them equally. Because of this, the children of each wife often become very protective of their mother, knowing that she has to compete with the other wives for their father's love and attention.

Thus a Somali household may commonly consist of one husband, four wives, and many children. In such cases, most wives prefer to live in a dwelling separate from their husband, rather than to share the same roof with another woman. The husband usually divides his time between the homes of his different wives.

DIVORCE

If a man wants a divorce, all he has to do is repeat, "I divorce you" three times to his wife. Once the couple is divorced, there is a three-month waiting period, to make sure the wife is not pregnant, before it is final.

If a woman wants to remarry her ex-husband, she must first marry and divorce another man. This problem does not arise too often, because couples usually divorce when the wife is too old to bear children, so the men are more likely to marry a younger woman than to remarry a former spouse.

A woman and her four children. Children of divorced parents usually stay with the mother.

SOMALI CHILDREN

As families and clans are very close-knit, children are a very visible part of Somali society. Somali parents love and cherish their children, but they are uncompromisingly strict with them and will punish them for misbehaving or for dishonoring the family name.

As divorce is common in Somalia, children often live with only one of their parents, usually the mother. Sometimes boys will live with the father and his new wife rather than with the mother, owing perhaps to clan loyalty.

Somali children grow up with many other children—siblings, cousins, and step-siblings. The adults in their lives include not just their parents, but also stepparents, grandparents, aunts, uncles, and sometimes great-grandparents.

Children are often regarded as bonds between different families and clans. Until a married woman bears a child, her loyalty remains more with her own family and clan. After a child is born, however, the wife gives her unreserved loyalty to her husband, and even her own relatives may develop strong ties to him and his family.

Somali girls taking home firewood for cooking.

69

STILL A LONG WAY TO GO FOR SOMALI WOMEN

Somalia remains a male-dominated society, but women have gained more freedom since 1969. Muslim law allows women to own, inherit, and pass on property. Although Somali women today aspire to positions primarily held by men, it remains difficult to obtain good jobs due to a lack of training and educational opportunities. In 2001 only some 26 percent of Somali women were literate.

On the whole, Somali society still expects women to be submissive toward men. Young women may advance in life only by exercising self-restraint, obeying and deferring to men, and displaying an attitude of self-denial.

A striking example of how women are treated as inferior is the cruel tradition of "circumcising" young girls. This custom originated as a way to keep young women "pure" until marriage. Female circumcision has been more accurately described as female genital mutilation (FGM) by the United Nations (UN). Some progressive Muslim leaders shun the practice of FGM and have ordered their followers to discontinue this barbaric act. Nonetheless, over 90 percent of Somali women have been made to undergo FGM. Even those Somali men who abhor this practice force their daughters to go through the ordeal because they are afraid that if they do not, no worthy man will want to marry them.

EDUCATION

The Somali educational system had improved a great deal under Siad Barre's regime, with emphasis being placed on the early education of children. Despite this, it did not bear any tangible results as the illiteracy rate remained around 85 percent until the early 1990s. The general state of anarchy during the 1992 civil war saw the regrettable collapse of Somalia's educational system.

One example of the general mayhem was that people forced their way into the national teacher-training center in Mogadishu and stole the desks. The school was shut down, which led to a shortage of trained teachers, and became a refugee camp. In the aftermath of the war, schools were closed and enrollment fell drastically. Many institutions of higher education were also destroyed. Among the surviving ones are the privately run Mogadishu University. In Somaliland, there are the Amoud University and Hargeysa University. By 1996 some schools were beginning to reopen.

Records show that in 2003, 19 percent of the total population could read and write. Two years later, it was estimated the figures nearly doubled to 37.8 percent for literacy. Nonetheless, the current literacy rate is still very low for young Somalis.

In 2006, the estimate was that only 26 percent of children were enrolled in primary schools. Pupils in the elementary grades learn reading, writing, languages, and mathematics. After primary school, students attend secondary schools or vocational schools to learn skills in industry, agriculture, and commerce.

Somali girls reading in a classroom. Gender segregation occurs in Somali schools, up to the university level.

Current efforts are being made to help more Somali children get a formal education. The UN International Children's Emergency Fund (UNICEF), with the support of the United Nations Educational, Scientific and Cultural Organization (UNESCO), members of the Somalia Aid Coordination Body's (SACB) Education Sectoral Committee, as well as other local committees, have come together on a project to reestablish and expand Somalia's primary school system.

Some of the progress includes developing a new primary school curriculum, printing new schoolbooks, standardizing learning materials, and starting a pilot mentoring project for 1,751 teachers.

IMAN: SOMALI SUPERMODEL

Iman was a well-known fashion model of the 1970s and 1980s. This Somali woman pursued an international modeling career and has appeared in American movies and television shows. In 1992, Iman married British rock star David Bowie. Currently, she is the CEO of Iman Cosmetics, Skincare and Fragrances, a beauty company with products for women of color.

Iman was born in Mogadishu in 1955 to a well-off family and grew up speaking five languages. She lived in Mogadishu until she was 17 years old. When Siad Barre took power in 1969, he detained all politicians. Her father, who was an ambassador for Somalia, was placed under house arrest. The whole family later sought political asylum in Tanzania.

She was studying political science at university in Nairobi, Kenya, when American photographer Peter Beard spotted her one day. Thus began her modeling career. She took the fashion world by storm and was hailed as the fashion world's next supermodel. Although Iman is now a U.S. citizen and resides there, she continues to be involved in charity work and issues that relate to Somalia and other African countries. In 2006, Iman became the global spokesperson for a campaign called Keep A Child Alive that supplies drugs to AIDS- or HIV-infected people in Africa and India.

Another fashion model who comes from Somalia is Waris Dirie. She is the cousin of Iman and a UN advocate for the abolition of female genital mutilation (FGM). Waris Dirie's family belongs to a nomadic tribe, and in 1965 she underwent female genital mutilation at five years of age. She ran away from Somalia at 13, to flee from an arranged marriage to a 60-year-old man. Her uncle helped her to move to London. Later, she was discovered by a photographer and began a modeling career. In 1998 she made a documentary, *Warie Dirie Speaks Out*, telling about her own experiences of undergoing FGM.

She has written three autobiographical books. The first one, *Desert Flower*, published in 1997, was a bestseller. A few years later, Waris Dirie visited her family, who still reside in Somalia, and wrote about this journey in another book, entitled *Desert Dawn*, published in 2002. The third book was *Desert Children*, in 2005. Today, she has stopped modeling and concentrates on her work campaigning against FGM.

RAVAGED CITIES

Over the past several decades, Somalia's cities have been ravaged by the civil wars. Many areas of Mogadishu, for instance, have been reduced to rubble. The conflicts between the north and south have brought grinding poverty to urban areas, as well as a population imbalance. Wealthy residents of the cities have fled to other countries, while rural citizens whose lives were disrupted by the civil wars have been moving steadily into the cities.

Today, Somalis are returning to the big towns and cities to rebuild their homes and offices, and to try to get on with life as best as they can. A very basic Somali home is the *arish* (AH-reesh), a rectangular building with timber, straw, dung, and mud walls and a pitched tin or thatched roof.

An improvement on the *arish* is the *baraca* (bah-RAH-kah), which is rectangular with cement floors and timber walls. If such a structure has stone or cement walls, the Somalis call it a *casa matoni* (KAH-sa ma-TOH-nee). Two other styles of Somali homes resemble those found in the West. The *casa moro* (KAH-sah MOH-roh) is a two-story house built of stone, in the Arabic style. The best houses in the cities are those built in the European style, with pitched tile roofs, walled courtyards, and stone walls.

A badly damaged part of Mogadishu. Cities in both the north and south were bombed during the years of civil war.

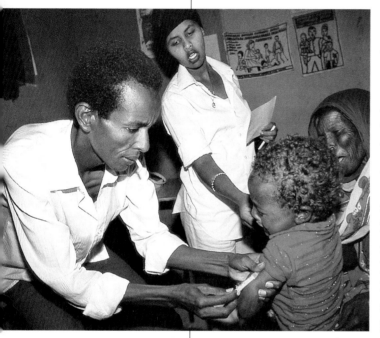

This child is lucky to have the attention of a doctor. Most Somalis have little access to health care.

HEALTH AND WELFARE

Although many aspects of Somali life improved after independence in 1960, the health and welfare of Somalis has declined significantly, mainly because of famine, wars, and floods. The government also failed to set up a workable health-care system for its citizens.

The end of socialism in Somalia brought about a further decline in medical attention. In the 1990s, doctors and hospital beds were in grave shortage. Today the continuing lack of health-care infrastructure is still keenly felt, because close to 80 percent of the inhabitants have little or no access to a basic health-care system.

One of the most common diseases in Somalia is tuberculosis. This affects many young men who work as camel herders. Because of their harsh working conditions, they contract the disease from their camels and then transmit it to others as they travel. The cities have been more successful in curbing tuberculosis than the smaller towns, because more nomads pass through the towns, making possible a widespread contagion.

More than half the population suffers from malaria or sickness caused by internal parasites transmitted in contaminated drinking water. But malnutrition is probably the most deadly scourge of all in Somalia, and droughts and famines have claimed the lives of thousands over the past few decades. In 2006, it was determined that 23 percent of the people suffered from malnutrition.

The *akals*, traditional homes of the nomadic and agricultural Somalis, are grouped together in a village.

MOVING HOUSE

Many rural Somalis live in makeshift homes or one-story houses with thatched roofs and dirt floors. The traditional rural home of the nomadic Somali tribes is a collapsible house or hut called an *akal* (ah-KAHL), which is made from pliable sticks tied together at the top and covered by a domed roof of hide or matting. Some nomads make these homes waterproof by weaving the matting on top very tightly. In slums and refugee camps, the huts are covered with cardboard, cloth, and flattened tin.

Nomads can erect or dismantle their homes in about two hours. Usually the *akals* are taken down by the women while the men begin the search for new pastures. The women also make utensils, weave ropes, fetch firewood, load and unload the camels with every move, care for the family's herd, and process the livestock products.

The nomads never reside in towns or cities. They pitch their tents or domed huts near pastures and sources of water needed by their herds. Once the water dries up, they take down their homes, load their belongings on their camels, and move on to the next spot.

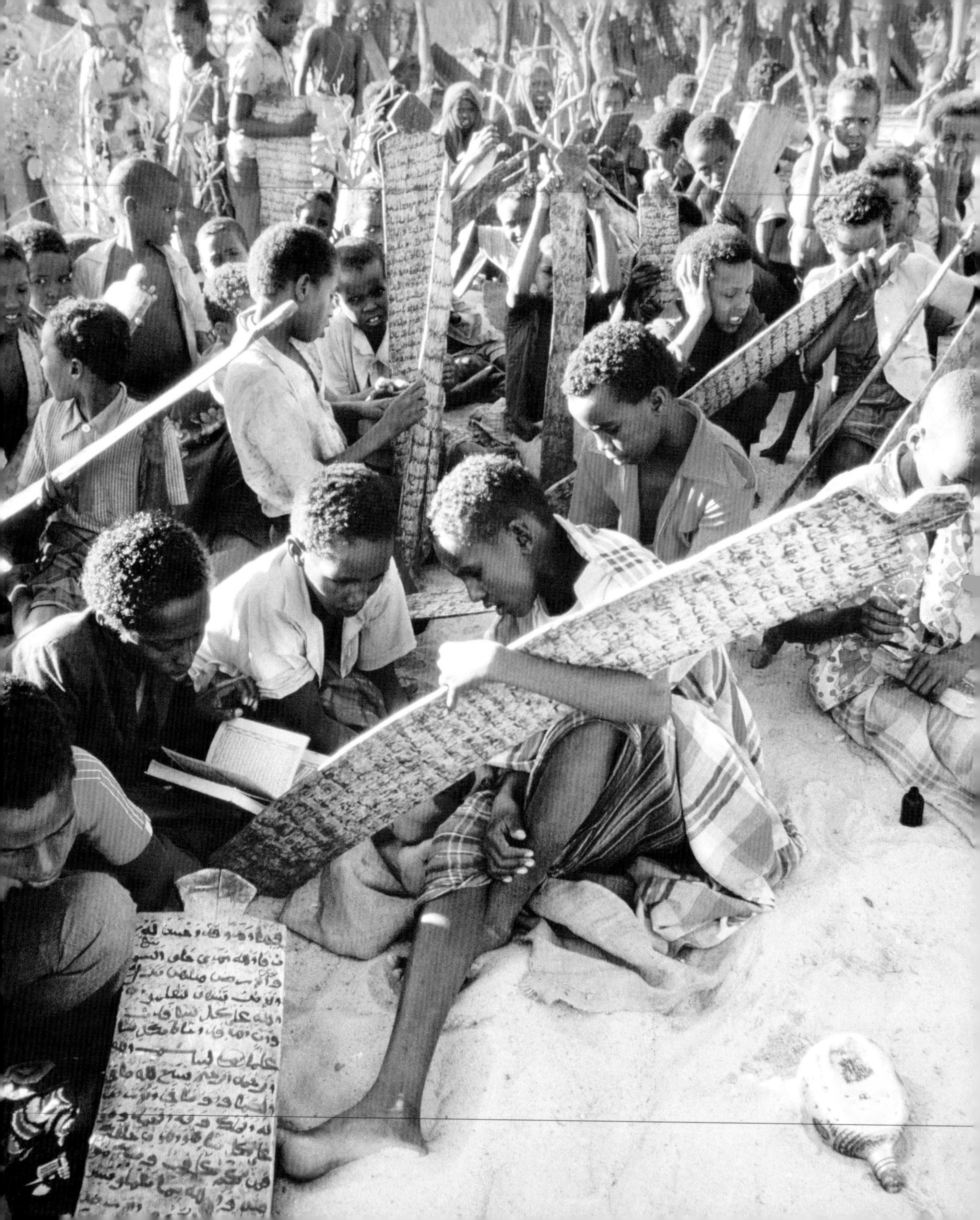

RELIGION

RELIGION IS ONE OF the most important aspects of a Somali's life. The state religion is Islam and almost all Somalis practice this faith. Christians make up less than 1 percent of the population.

Islam has an overwhelming influence on everyday life. Schools teach the religion, and its precepts dictate marriage and divorce laws. Nearly all Muslims in Somalia are Sunnis, who believe that their religious leaders should be elected by the people. As Somalia has yet to have a functioning national legal system, some conflicts are arbitrated by Sharia or Islamic law. The Union of Islamic Courts (UIC) also imposed Sharia law when it controlled the southern part of Somalia.

Above: **This mosque in Mogadishu was built with the help of the Kuwaiti government.**

Opposite: **Somali children recite lines from the Islamic holy book, the Koran.**

The other sect of Muslims, the Shiites, split with the Sunnis after the death of the Prophet Muhammad. The Shiites believe that only the descendants of Muhammad should become religious leaders, claiming that these men possess superior qualities.

Somali Muslims, although following the same beliefs as other Muslims, have modified Islam to accommodate their indigenous beliefs. For instance, contrary to other Sunnis, Somalis believe that their leaders possess the power to bless and curse individuals. They call this *baruka* (bah-ROO-kah) and believe it to be a God-given power entrusted to both religious and secular leaders.

THE FIVE PILLARS OF ISLAM

The Prophet Muhammad, who founded the religion of Islam, was born around A.D. 570 to a prominent family during a time of civil unrest. As a young man he married and became a merchant trader.

Muhammad first encountered God through the archangel Gabriel at a cave near Mecca, where he used to pray and meditate. He was given and then ordered to memorize and recite the lines of the Koran, the Islamic holy book.

When Muhammad told his wife of this experience, she became his first convert. Over the years of his life, Muhammad converted thousands of people to Islam, and by the time he died, almost everyone in the Arab world had embraced the faith.

All over the world, Muslims follow strict principles called the Five Pillars of Islam. The first pillar is the *shahada* (sha-HAH-dah), a creed that every Muslim must proclaim. The *shahada* states: "There is no God but Allah, and Muhammad is His Prophet."

The second pillar requires Muslims to pray five times a day, each time facing the holy city of Mecca in Saudi Arabia. Muslims need not go to a mosque to pray but may pray wherever they happen to be. Many Somali Muslims therefore carry a prayer mat with them to use for their five daily prayer sessions.

Zakat (ZAH-kaht), or the giving of alms to the less fortunate, is the third pillar of Islam. The fourth pillar is to observe the holy month of Ramadan, during which Muslims must fast from dawn to dusk.

The fifth pillar of Islam is the obligation to make a pilgrimage to Mecca, if one is financially and physically able to do so, at least once in a lifetime.

THE KORAN

The Islamic holy book is called the Koran. Many of the stories found in the Jewish Torah and the Old Testament of the Christian Bible can also be found in the Koran. The three religions are closely related.

Muslims believe that their scriptures are the most authentic, although they acknowledge that the Jewish and Christian holy books are also revelations from God. The Koran, like the Bible, teaches that both heaven and hell exist. Both the holy books stress a belief in God, and both relate the story of the creation of humankind in the Garden of Eden.

In the Koran, Muslims, Jews, and Christians are all regarded as "children of the book."

SUNNI MUSLIM SECTS

Most Somalis are Sunnis who follow the Sufi school of belief. Within the Sufi school are three divisions, or sects—the Qadiriya, the Salihiya, and the Ahmediya.

The Qadiriya is the oldest sect of Islam and was founded in Baghdad in 1166. Somalis became associated with this sect in 1883. The first Qadiriya leader in Somalia was Sheikh Abdarahman al Zeilawi, who preached the faith in the northern regions and in Ethiopia. At the same time, different leaders introduced the Qadiriya sect to the southern Somali regions.

The Qadiriya are considered to be highly spiritual people because they are reclusive and remove themselves from modern concerns.

Muhammad ibn Salih founded the Salihiya sect in 1887 in Ethiopia. Within a couple of years, this sect was gaining followers in Somalia. Along the Shabelle River, a man named Sheikh Muhammad Guled ar Rashidi became a regional leader of the Salihiya sect. The Salihiyas are regarded as the most fanatical sect of Sunni Muslims in Somalia

The third group of Somali Sunnis, the Ahmediya, was founded by Sayyid Ahmad ibn Idris al Fasi of Mecca. The sect was introduced to Somalia at the end of the 19th century by Sheikh Ali Maye. The Ahmediyas conduct rituals that include simple prayers and hymns, during which followers fall into a trance. Ahmediyan leaders concentrate on teaching the Koran and the Hadith, which is a book of legends about the Prophet Muhammad.

CATHEDRALS AND MOSQUES

During the colonial period, at the height of Italian influence, the Italians built a Roman Catholic cathedral in Mogadishu, which is one of the few Christian places of worship in the country. The few Catholics in Somalia come under the Diocese of Mogadishu. Just next door to this cathedral is a mosque. In fact, mosques can be found all over Somalia, especially in the larger cities. Some of them are architecturally spectacular. In Mogadishu, local residents believe that the Sheikh Abdul Aziz mosque, with its distinctive round minaret, emerged from the sea. Outside the cities there are smaller mosques, as well as the remains of ancient mosques.

Children being given religious instruction.

RITES FOR PILGRIMS TO PERFORM IN MECCA

Mecca, the birthplace of the Prophet Muhammad, is in the Hejaz province of Saudi Arabia. Certain strict rules have to be observed when making the pilgrimage to this holy city. Muslims always arrive in Mecca on foot. Those who live far away may need to take a plane to Saudi Arabia and continue the rest of the journey on foot.

When pilgrims are about 6 miles (10 km) away from Mecca, they divide into separate groups of the same sex. To carry out the pilgrimage rites, they have to be in a state of ritual purity. They do so by performing an initial ritual bathing and cleansing as well as putting on suitable clothing befitting their pilgrimage. Some of the regulations they must follow when performing the hajj include refraining from marital relations, not shaving or cutting their nails, and not fighting or arguing with others.

Once they arrive in Mecca, they must go through a number of rites in a specific order. First the pilgrims purify themselves a second time by bathing in the forenoon; adorning themselves appropriately, and making a statement of intention to perform the hajj. They then spend the day at Mina and offer five prayers there.

When the sun rises, they head to Arafat and stay until the sun sets, praying and glorifying Allah and asking for his forgiveness. After sunset, they head to Muzdalifah, stay overnight and continue with their prayers. Shortly before sunrise, the pilgrims head back to Mina and use special stones to throw at three pillars in Mina, signifying that they are stoning the "devils." Next they slaughter a sacrificial animal. Afterward, the men will either shave or trim their hair while the women clip their hair about the length of a fingertip shorter. At this juncture, the pilgrims take off their special garments and are allowed to wear other clothing.

Later the pilgrims head to Mecca and climb to the tops of Mount Marwah and Mount Safa. This is followed by running or jogging between the two mountains for seven times. After completing this step, the pilgrims return to Mina and repeat the action of stoning the three pillars signifying the devil. At each pillar, the participants throw seven consecutive pebbles.

Lastly, the return to Mecca will end with the circling of the Ka'bah, a black cube-shaped monument in the Grand Mosque of Mecca, seven times. The circling of the Ka'bah will mark the conclusion of the hajj's rites. The pilgrim can also make a recommended visit to the Prophet's Mosque in Medina, but that is optional and not part of the hajj itself.

NOTED SAINTS IN SOMALIA

Muslim Somalis venerate their own saints in addition to worshipping Allah. Tombs of Muslim saints can be found all over Somalia. These saints are actually Somali holy men who become revered as saints after they die. These holy men had given up their worldly possessions and went about the land preaching the word of Allah. He earns the title of saint upon his death if he is deemed to have been deeply spiritual and to have performed acts of kindness and mercy to those in need.

His widow has to build a small mosque over his burial site and care for his grave. Somali Muslims believe that the power of a saint is at its strongest during the month after his death. At such a time, believers gather at his grave to pray and to listen to verses from the Koran. These devout visitors often tear a piece off their clothes, tie the shred of cloth around the railing of the tomb, and promise to perform a good deed if the saint grants their wish.

Both adults and children are familiar with the names of their saints. Children are told about these saints by the village storyteller or learn about them in school.

One of the most well-known Somali saints is Sheikh Muhr Mohammed from Hargeysa, who wrote religious poetry in Arabic and translated traditional Islamic hymns from Arabic to Somali. During a severe drought, the Somalis asked Sheikh Mohammed to pray for rain. Within hours, rain fell on the region.

Two other eminent Somali saints are Sheikh Abd ar Rahman Abdullah and Sheikh Ali Maye. Sheikh Abdullah had a reputation for sanctity and the gift of prophecy. Today his followers still circulate his writings as well as visit his tomb in Mogadishu. Regarding the saint Sheikh Ali Maye, it is said that one day he met a young boy who could not speak or read.

EVIL SPIRITS IN FOLK BELIEFS

In Somalia, as in many other African nations, folklore is an inseparable part of religion. For example, Somalis believe that when someone gives them the "evil eye," it causes a malevolent spirit to enter their soul. Victims may suffer from sneezing, coughing, vomiting, or skin rashes. The only cure for this would be for a religious leader to hold a ceremony in which he recites verses of the Koran, makes the sufferer drink water, and bathes him in perfume.

Another belief among Somalis is possession by an evil spirit called the *zar* (zahr), causing fainting and hysteria. The victims are always women who have grievances against their husbands. If a woman is possessed by this evil spirit, her community holds a religious ceremony to exorcise the spirit.

A third type of spirit is called the *gelid* (GAY-lid). A person so possessed usually has injured another person, and the remedy for this is a ceremony consisting of readings from the Koran.

It is also believed that people who are poor, helpless, or injured are protected by Allah, who gives them special powers that they may use to help others. Such powers can also be used to hurt others. As a result, Somalis believe that they have to be kind to someone less fortunate, or else they could be cursed by them.

The saint then slapped the boy on the head, and the boy began to speak and read fluent Arabic.

There is a well-known tale among Somalis of the half-blind saint, Sheikh Ali Gure. He was once traveling with three attendants when he suddenly asked them to leave him alone for a few hours. A short time later, his attendants returned to the spot where they had left him sitting on the ground, but he was not there and they could not find him.

Eventually the sheikh materialized at the same spot and told his attendants a wondrous story. It appeared that some Muslims at sea were in trouble because their boat had sustained damage. They prayed to Allah to mend their boat, and through Allah's power, Sheikh Gure was sent to them. He was able to place a board over the hole in their boat, making it watertight. Then, by that same power, he returned to his original spot on the ground.

MOURNING PERIOD FOR SOMALI WIDOWS

When a Somali woman's husband dies, she must adhere to a strict Muslim ritual. She is to remain in mourning for four months and 10 days. During this time, Islam dictates that she must wear only white clothes and remain at home. She cannot touch grease or a man's hand, and she can only shower and wash her hair once or twice a week. The widow must save all of the hairs from her comb and keep her nail clippings.

At the end of the mourning period, several sheikhs and two or three religious women arrive at the widow's home. The women take the widow into the bathroom where they wash her hair and body and dress her in new clothes of the widow's favorite color.

Once the widow is clean and dressed, everyone, including the sheikhs, go outside the house to bury her hair combings and nail clippings. The sheikhs then pray for the widow and her dead husband. After they have read aloud parts of the Koran, the ceremony ends, and everyone celebrates the end of the mourning period.

RELIGION AND POLITICS

Religion has always played an important role in the governing of Somalia. After gaining political independence in 1960 from their colonial masters, Somalis were granted the right to freedom of religion. Subsequently, Islam was declared the state religion.

Secular authorities with new fiscal powers gradually took over legal and educational responsibilities, and the role of religious functionaries decreased.

The 1969 revolution and the introduction of Scientific Socialism substantially and drastically changed the position of religious leaders.

Siad Barre insisted that Scientific Socialism, which was his version of socialism, was compatible with Islamic principles. At the same time, he also condemned atheism, and religious leaders were warned not to meddle in politics.

Siad Barre and his new government instituted legal changes that some religious figures saw as contrary to Islamic precepts. For example, in 1975, Siad Barre granted women a number of new rights, including the right to inherit, and he even went as far as citing the Koran for his decision. It seemed to some people that Somali women would now happily have equal status in a predominately male-oriented Somali society.

Not surprisingly, religious leaders protested strongly against this new law. The government's response to them was ruthless. Ten religious leaders from Mogadishu were executed. After the execution, other religious chiefs kept a low profile and seemed to accommodate themselves to Siad Barre's rule and legislative governance.

When the socialist government collapsed in 1991, religious leaders actively resumed their political role in Somali society.

In the void left by the absence of a central government, new Muslim sects and parties arose. One particularly powerful Islamic group is the Union of Islamic Courts (UIC), which controlled the capital, Mogadishu, and many parts of the south until December 2006.

These Muslims praying outdoors have carefully created an enclosed prayer area marked by stones and boulders.

LANGUAGE

MANY SOMALIS ARE FLUENT in five or more languages. Because the Koran is written in Arabic, many Somali Muslims are familiar with this language. Some Somalis also speak French, Italian, or English because of past colonial rule. Even so, the official language is Somali, which belongs to a linguistic group called Lowland Eastern Cushitic. It is also related to some of the languages of Ethiopia, Djibouti, and Kenya.

Although the written form of Somali was introduced only in 1972, the spoken form has been used for centuries. The Somali tongue resembles languages spoken in nearby African countries. Even during British and Italian control of Somalia, the people continued to speak Somali while learning their colonial masters' languages. The Somali tongue has several dialects that vary according to region. The most widely used of these is Common Somali. The areas between the Jubba and Shabelle rivers as well as some of the communities of the coastal cities of the south have other dialects.

Before 1972 English and Italian were the two official languages of the government. Somalis who spoke either of these, therefore, had better career opportunities in government and business circles.

When the Somali script was finally established in 1972, the government required all its officials to learn it. Attempts were made also to teach urban and rural Somalis how to read and write the language. These attempts were not very successful, and the country still has a high illiteracy rate.

Above: **The sign above the doorway of a bookshop in Mogadishu shows the new written style of Somali language.**

Opposite: **A boy holding a writing tablet inscribed with Arabic script.**

THE SACRED TONGUE

Most Somalis are fluent in Arabic, or at least understand it. Arabic is one of the official languages of Somalia and the liturgical language of Islam. It originated in Saudi Arabia in the mid-fourth century, but was not recorded in writing until centuries later.

Arabic is difficult to learn, as it is very different from most other languages. Somalis, like other Muslims, consider Arabic to be Allah's (God's) language. There are three tongues in Arabic; the one known to Somalis is standard Arabic, which is a modernized version of classical Arabic, the language of the Koran. Arabic script, with its beautiful artistic calligraphy, looks very different from the script of most modern languages.

When the government was deciding on a written form of Somali, many religious leaders were disappointed that the form eventually picked resembled English rather than the Arabic script.

NAMES

Somalis have long names that tell a lot about their lineage. When a child is born, the parents give him or her a personal name. After this, the names given are the child's father's personal name, the personal name of the father's father, and so on, up to the name of the founder of the subclan and then, finally, the name of the clan family.

Somali children heading off to school. They learn to read and write at least two languages.

SOMALI WORDS AND PHRASES

Many Somali words have Arabic origins. Over 90 percent of Somalis are Muslims, but their language is quite different from Arabic and even has regional variations. The difference between Common Somali and the other tongues is somewhat similar to that between Spanish and Portuguese. As is the case between these two European languages, the words in the Somali tongues have basically the same roots but are pronounced differently according to region. Words may also have a different prefix or suffix. Some of the most widely used Common Somali words are:

English	Somali	English	Somali
one	*kow*	yes	*ha*
two	*laba*	no	*maya*
three	*sader*	food	*ahnto*
four	*afar*	bread	*roti*
five	*shan*	rice	*baris*
ten	*toban*	meat	*hillip*
hundred	*bogol*	water	*beeyu*
thousand	*kuhn*	tea	*shah*
Good morning	*Subah wanaqsan*	Where is?	*Hage?*
Good afternoon	*Galeb wanaqsan*	How much?	*Waa imissa?*
Good evening	*Habeen wanaqsan*	toilet	*musghul*

People in the same families and clans tend to live near one another in cities and towns. When a Somali visits a strange town, he or she can always track down relatives or clan family simply by asking where a certain family or clan name can be found. Families always welcome their relatives into their homes, even if they have never seen them before.

Not only is a person's name helpful in locating hospitable relatives, it tells a Somali how closely he or she is related to others simply by comparing their names. The more names they have in common, the more closely they are related. For instance, brothers and sisters have the same names except for their first or personal names. Cousins hold different first and second names, and these are their personal names as well as their fathers' personal names. But their other names will be the same. People who are related only through the clan family have different names except for the very last name. Because their names are so long, Somalis rarely use their full names.

There are between 15 to 20 million speakers of the Somali language.

WORDPLAY AND HUMOR

Since Somalia's written language was created only in 1972, prior to that, Somalis relied on strong oral literary traditions, their memory, and verbal skills to record and recount their history and to disseminate important news. Oral traditions continue to play an important part even today. People earned the respect of others by mastering such communication skills. Somali society has always judged those in power, such as political or religious leaders, on their ability to use the Somali language to its full advantage. These leaders are expected to use rhetoric skillfully through poetry, vivid words, and alliteration.

Above: **This man is displaying a placard written in both English and Somali, stating the aim of his group, the United Somalia Salvation Youth.**

Opposite: **A group of women in town have a chat before doing the morning's marketing.**

Negotiating is a delicate skill because Somalis do not like either to be blunt when asking for a favor or to receive a direct refusal. Therefore, prior to asking for help in performing a task or cooperating on a project, a Somali will approach the subject indirectly to discover the other person's general attitude. If the person responds favorably, then the Somali will state his request. If it seems that the person is not inclined to agree to the request, the embarrassment of a refusal would then be avoided.

The use of humor is another important communication skill in everyday language. Somalis, like people of other nations, use humor quite often to soften awkward situations. A person who is just learning the language would probably be lost without a full understanding of the way Somalis use verbal wit for amusement.

90

MANNERS OF GREETING

When Somali men meet one another, they always shake hands. A woman usually waits until a man extends his hand before offering her own.

Usually men and women will not have any physical contact when meeting, unless they happen to be members of the same family.

When greeting one another, family members hug and kiss, as people do in other countries. Members of the same sex often embrace or kiss one another on the cheek.

NONVERBAL BEHAVIOR AND GESTURES

Although Somalia is an African nation, its religious and cultural affinities have tended to be closer to Arab nations. Most Somalis know Arabic well enough to recite the Koran from memory.

Even nonverbal communication in Somalia has been influenced by that of the Arab nations. The following are universal Arabic gestures, used by Arabs and Somalis alike:

- Moving the right hand up and down with the palm facing down means "Be quiet."
- Holding the right hand out while opening and closing the hand means "Come here."
- Moving the right hand away from the body with the palm facing down means "Go away."
- Placing the right hand on the heart after shaking hands signifies sincerity.
- Raising the eyebrows with a tilted-back head or shaking the right forefinger from right to left means "No."

ARTS

SOMALIA HAS A RICH CULTURAL HISTORY, going back to ancient Egyptian times. The Egyptian influence began when Queen Hatshepsut of Egypt sent men to Somalia, then known as the Land of Punt, to obtain incense, ivory, skins, and spices. By the seventh century, Arab and Persian traders were also making their presence felt.

By the 10th century, Arab and Persian influences were reflected in Somali artwork such as swords, daggers, marble objects, and pottery. Examples of these early objects can be seen today in museums of the big cities. Fine examples of craftwork, including jewelry, woven mats, and drums made from animal skins and tree fibers, are also on display.

The Somalis did not have a written form of poetry until recently, but their oral skills of poetry recitation are widely practiced, and they have passed down their poems through generations.

Left: **Local villagers gathered together to have a traditional dance.**

Opposite: **Somali women are skilled at weaving intricate mats and rugs from natural fibers.**

ISLAM AND SOMALI ART

Islam has been the most significant influence on Somali art over the centuries. Because most Somali artists were Muslims, their religious beliefs are reflected in their art.

Islam prohibits the portrayal of humans or animals in religious art, so artistic subjects tend to be flowers, vases, creatures of the imagination, or calligraphy. Colors are bright and vibrant, a favorite being Mohammed blue (cobalt blue)—a color that the Chinese in the 13th century developed for their porcelain in honor of the Prophet.

Islamic art is rich with intricate designs, and these often appear on paintings, pottery, ceramics, tiles, and carpets. Some Muslim artists design wall hangings for private homes, incorporating verses from the Koran. Because the Arabic script is so beautiful, such wall hangings are very attractive and often are considered works of art.

Arabic script of words from the Koran: "The sun never eclipses the sky."

SO MUCH MORE EXPRESSIVE TO USE CAMEL TALK

Camels are so vital to the Somalis that disputes over them have often caused rivalry and feuds between communities and clans. As such, the animal has a special place in the literary tradition of the country. Poets use what are known as "camel metaphors" to express feelings of love, hate, jealousy, and desire.

Even ordinary Somalis have a repertoire of "camel expressions" reflecting the importance of the camel in their daily lives. For instance, there is an area in Somalia called Candho-qoy (KAHN-doh-koy), meaning "the place of moist udders," while another word, *geel-weyta* (GEEL-WEY-tah), means "the place that weakens animals." Scholars call their research *raadra* (RAAH-drah), literally "to trace lost animals." Problems set out in a school textbook are called *laylis* (LAH-yis), which refers to "breaking of a young camel."

During the 1970s and 1980s the Islamic influence was absent from works of art. This was because the socialist regime had ordered artists to incorporate socialist propaganda into their work instead.

ALL THE WORLD'S A STAGE

Most dramatic works performed in Somalia before the 1950s originated in other countries, but for the last 50 years or so, Somalis have been writing their own plays. Somalis are natural performers and have produced and directed these plays at the now defunct National Theater in Mogadishu or at theaters in other cities.

Drama was part of the school curriculum in British Somaliland, with an emphasis on stagecraft. From that, Somalis graduated to producing plays in town halls and to writing their own plays, including drama groups for women. In Italian Somaliland, the Italians helped Somalis write and produce plays, thus encouraging local talents.

After the written Somali script was developed, plays began to be written in Somali. Today playwrights write in Somali, Arabic, English, and Italian. A few of Somalia's foremost dramatists are Hassan Mumin, Mohamed Ali Kaariye, and Ali Sugule. Novelists and playwrights Maxamed Daahir Afrax and Nuruddin Farah are also equally recognized at home and abroad. Farah was awarded the Neustadt International Prize for Literature in 1998.

A group of happy children anticipating a tale from a storyteller.

ART OF STORYTELLING

Storytelling is a traditional art in Somalia. From one generation to the next, those who cannot read or write but have a gift for storytelling are able to pass on both true and fictional anecdotes of value. One well-known Somali story is of a man called Gurgati and his two sons.

Gurgati lived in the countryside with his family. When the land was hit by drought, Gurgati asked his two elder sons to go and find water for their goats, sheep, camels, and cows. The sons, who had never been on such a mission before, asked Gurgati what they should do if they could not find water and wandered too far away from home.

Gurgati's reply was that they should continue until they found water, no matter how far from home that took them. They must walk in the morning, but stop to rest when it got hot, then continue walking in the evening. Gurgati warned them that if they saw a dead animal or anything else they could eat, they should eat only enough to keep them alive and not fill their stomach or take the meat with them. When they finally found food and water, Gurgati added, they should then vomit up everything they had eaten, because the animal carcass they had eaten would not have been fresh. They should then wash themselves. The two sons set out. They traveled for many days without finding water.

Finally, they spotted a dead animal and started to eat some of the meat. The older brother stuffed himself, but the younger one ate only enough to satisfy his hunger. The older brother also decided to take some of the meat with him to eat along the way, but the younger son once again heeded his father's warning.

The younger son was surprised and disappointed that his brother was so blatantly disobeying their father, but he stayed with his brother on their quest to find food and water for the family.

Eventually, the brothers found pastures, inhabited by nomads, with both water and food. The younger brother duly threw up the unclean meat in his stomach, and he remembered to wash himself before eating the food set out before them by a nomad family. But he refused to eat from the same plate as his brother, whom he regarded as unclean. The father was told this whole story when the two sons returned home. Gurgati was furious with his elder son for disobeying and disgracing him, and threw him out of the house. The son became poorer and poorer, traveling from town to town in search of food and work. Eventually he got married and had children, and his children had children of their own, and so on, through the generations.

Some Somalis today still believe that their countrymen from the so-called "lower castes" are descendants of this eldest son of Gurgati. The story, however, ends on the note that although the two classes are separated by the acts of that distant forefather, all Somalis belong to the same family, united by blood, religion, and language.

A little boy scoops up water, a precious commodity in Somalia and one often featured in poetry, songs, and stories.

97

POETRY AND DANCES

Poems recited to villagers and small town residents often had the power to bring about important political changes and could even start or end wars.

Somalis have the gift of poetry, and poetry is one of the country's greatest artistic achievements. For centuries, it has been not just an art form but also a political and cultural tool.

If a community was confronted with a problem, tribal leaders met to decide on what action to take. After a decision had been reached, the wise men passed it on to the local poet. The poet, who commanded great respect in the community, would then compose a poem. Such a poem, one that conveyed the decision of the leaders to their people, was called a *gabaye* (gah-bah-YAH).

Once the *gabaye* was created, the town or village community would gather together to hear the poem being delivered. The poet gave the *gabaye* only once to the community. Subsequent recitations were left to poetry reciters. These poetry reciters are tasked to repeat the *gabayes* composed by the village or town poet, and they must deliver the poem perfectly, exactly word for word. Reciters need to have excellent memories, because some *gabayes* could be more than a hundred words long. As the *gabaye* is also an official order from the leaders, poetry reciters are not allowed to make any facial expressions during their recitations or to act out the story in any way or to emphasize any words or phrases. The poetry reciter's role was to repeat the poem not only to the poet's community but to other communities as well, and always with perfect accuracy. Such poems would often include details about local history, current affairs, and the community's customs.

Somalis also compose poems to commemorate significant events in their private lives—to express their love for someone, to propose a marriage or to end one, to celebrate the birth of a child, or to mourn the death of a loved one.

Public events such as political debates also require that poetry be composed and recited. Such poetry is highly competitive, as the best poet not only wins honor and prestige for his clan but wins livestock for himself as well.

Some of these public occasions may also call for dancers to perform. Somalis are fond of dancing, and they are good both at improvising and at performing traditional dances.

But the art of oral poetry may be in danger of fading away. The nomadic Somalis are beginning to learn to read and write, which means they will no longer need to rely exclusively on getting their information from the local poet and the poetry reciters. Radio broadcasting has also led to the ability to disseminate information quickly and to a much larger audience. Messages from one community to another can now be freely transmitted over the airwaves.

Some Somali poets and authors, like Ahmed Farah Ali "Idaja" and Sheik Jaamac Cumar Cisse, are presently trying to collect all of the poems and stories still being told in the oral tradition and write them down, to preserve this heritage for future generations. These transcripts of poems and tales may someday become the classical Somali literature.

Important poets like Maxamed Xaashi Dhamac "Gaarriye," Mohamed Ibrahim Warsame "Hadrawi," and Cali Xuseen Xirsi have also kept

A group of dancers at a public festival.

Heello *(HE-low)* *is a popular genre of music that is influenced by Somali poetry.*

99

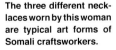

The three different necklaces worn by this woman are typical art forms of Somali craftsworkers.

the spirit of Somali poetry alive in the written form. Some of their published works cover wide-ranging social and political subjects such as nuclear weapons, patriotism, and protests against the import of foreign cars.

JEWELRY AND ARTIFACTS

Somalis are fond of wearing ornamental jewelry on festive occasions. Silver is the preferred metal, as many believe that silver is the "pure" metal blessed by the Prophet Muhammad, and that gold belongs to the devil and brings bad luck.

Since few Somalis can afford even silver, most jewelry is made of colored beads of wood, stone, or glass.

Traditionally, Somali women make the pottery and do it without a potter's wheel. They hollow out a ball of clay and mold it into shape. Once the object is baked, the women use dyes from plants to add design and color.

Somalis, particularly the women, also make decorative wooden cups. Some of these wooden goblets are used for drinking, but others are fashioned to hold powder and other cosmetic items. They tend to be well designed, featuring motifs of animals, boats, or huts. Both men and women are adept at woodcarving; examples of their skill include items such as spoons or boxes for holding medicine, jewelry, and other accessories. They also carve dried gourds.

Most rural Somalis eat their food with their right hand instead of spoons or forks, yet many do have finely carved serving spoons which are seen as symbols of wealth. If a family possesses such utensils, they are only for display to indicate their success or status and not for use. However,

The modest stone facade of a building in Hammawein, an old quarter of Mogadishu.

some wealthy urban Somalis do actually use spoons functionally rather than just for display.

The spoon is also a symbol of domesticity, often given to a young woman who has given birth to her first child. This is to symbolize the new phase of her life. Most of these spoons are made of wood and have decorative handles, but can be made of silver or ivory.

VARIED ARCHITECTURE

Traditional dwellings in rural areas are small modest homes, the domed hut or *akal* being the most common. Architecture in the cities is more varied and may be traditional or modern, lavish or modest. Some are quaint structures from the past, many are bland stone buildings suitable for the hot climate, and yet others are modern buildings in the Western style.

It is unfortunate that within the last few decades bombs and gunfire have destroyed much of the most historic and beautiful architecture of the cities of Somalia, especially those buildings along the coast.

LEISURE

FAMINES AND CIVIL WARS have curtailed Somalis' enjoyment of leisure pastimes over the past several decades, but they still take part in various activities whenever they can. In the north, the mountains provide opportunities for good hiking, rock climbing, and animal watching.

Swimming is popular among Somalis living in the fertile region between the two main rivers, Shabelle and Jabelle—although swimmers have to watch out for hungry predatory creatures such as crocodiles. Swimming is a bit safer on the coast, but even there, the danger of sharks lurks if swimmers venture out too far.

In rural areas people tend to be sociable. Visiting neighbors in the clan community and gathering together to make handicrafts are favorite pastimes for rural women. The children enjoy playing games and listening to stories told by their elders. All across the country, Somalis engage in active sports such as running, soccer, basketball, and boxing. Until recently, popular pastimes in the cities included going to plays and movies.

Left: **The woman in the foreground has just been calling on her neighbors, a typical leisure activity for Somali women.**

Opposite: **A group of Somali boys playing a friendly game of basketball in an outdoor court.**

COFFEE BREAKS

Somali women get together as often as they can, usually in their homes or in stores. Until a few years ago, a Somali female seldom entered a restaurant. If she did, she was assumed to be a woman of ill repute. To avoid misunderstandings, Somali women to this day tend to avoid going into restaurants.

Whenever a Somali housewife finds herself with some time in the morning, she visits her friends and relatives. She stays to chat and to have a glass of coffee or fruit juice. Such visits typically last half an hour, which is considered long enough to be enjoyable but not intrusive.

Men in the towns and cities socialize mainly in restaurants and coffeehouses. These places are full at all times of the day, with different groups of men eating, drinking coffee, or simply talking.

These Somalis make the most of their leisure time, drinking coffee together at a friend's house.

GOING TO MARKET

All Somalis, especially the women, enjoy going to the market. It's where they do the family shopping, meet up with their friends, and get the chance to pick up some bargains. For rural women living far from a town, a trip to the market is a full day's event.

Somali women do their marketing early in the morning. The outdoor markets are the best places to find fresh fruit and vegetables, as well as meat and milk. The vendors sit in the sun all day long to sell their goods. When a Somali woman wants to buy milk, she brings along tin containers with handles. She goes taste-testing from vendor to vendor, and once she finds the milk she likes, she fills all of her tins with the milk.

The marketplace is usually a square in the middle of town. In the larger towns and cities, little stores are located all around it. Somalis love to spend time examining the wares in these shops, which predominately sell handicrafts.

Bakara Market is the main place to shop in Mogadishu. It is the busiest market in the capital city, with shops surrounding it displaying pottery cups and bowls and handicrafts made of camel bone, wood, or fabric.

A colorful market scene in one of the towns. Going marketing is an important social experience for many Somalis.

LEATHERWORK AND WEAVING

Making handicrafts is a favorite pastime for Somali women, who have made beautiful items for centuries. Traditional leather objects such as sandals, charms, cowhide beds, and pitchers for water and milk are fashioned by crafters living in rural communities. Long hours are spent making intricate designs in the leather. In the cities, leather goods are produced mainly in tanneries and leather factories.

During the colonial period, Italians taught the Somalis modern leatherworking techniques and helped them build factories. Such factories now turn out decorative leather items, including purses, sandals, and jackets with fringes. They also produce coats and footwear from animal pelts, which are popular with the wealthier urban Somalis. Somalis also enjoy weaving, which is an everyday affair for young Somali girls. They learn this skill from their mothers.

Woven products such as rugs and fabrics are sometimes made from homemade cotton thread. To make the thread, they remove the soft fluff from around cotton seeds and spin the fluff into thin thread or heavier yarn. They dye the bundles of threads and hang them out to dry, after which they arrange the threads on a loom and weave rugs or lengths of cloth. Making mats involves a different process. First the women pull bark from the trees, pound it, and then soak it in water. Once the bark is soft, the women weave it into mats.

Other local products include pipes, candlesticks, beadwork, shell necklaces, small carvings, and products made from ivory and tortoiseshell. Handicraft making is not only an enjoyable leisure activity for Somalis; it is also a source of income for them.

GETTING INTO A SOMALI CINEMA WITHOUT A TICKET

Before the Union of Islamic Courts (UIC) shut down cinemas in the territory it controlled, movie theaters in Somalia tended to be of two kinds—either an open-air theater consisting of long benches and a screen, or an enclosed hall. In an indoor cinema, women and children traditionally sit on the lower level, while the men occupy the upper level.

Under the socialist regime, trying to purchase a ticket at a Somali movie theater was an interesting experience. Since Siad Barre's government controlled the cinemas and required their proprietors to turn over all their profits, many unhappy cinema owners would tell their staff not to issue too many tickets, so that they did not have a record of having sold these to customers. That is why some moviegoers were not issued any tickets in spite of the fact that they had paid for them. In this way, the owners kept most of their box-office proceeds.

Before the UIC ban on films, Somali children enjoyed trips to the movies and watching American and European action films, even if they did not understand what was being said. Most Somali parents do not like their children to go to the cinema, as they do not approve of Western movies, which they think depict too much sex and violence.

Men using simple fishing lines attempt to catch fish off the coast of Mogadishu. Boys often accompany their fathers and learn from them during these outings.

FUN AT THE BEACHES

Friday is the official rest day for Somalis. On that day and on holidays, many people take their families to the beaches, especially to those in Mogadishu. They play soccer, stroll along the sand, run in the surf, or brave the shark-infested waters of the Indian Ocean to swim. Children enjoy building sand castles or playing games along the beach.

The most popular sandy stretch in Mogadishu is Gezira beach. There are numerous isolated coves along the coast that can provide complete privacy, although these sheltered nooks are not protected from sharks, and swimming can be quite risky.

The waters of Somalia are also home to many other living creatures that make swimming less attractive than it would otherwise be. The scorpion fish is a beautiful, colorful fish with zebralike stripes—and poisonous dorsal spines. This fish, unlike sharks, will not attack unless provoked. Another dangerous fish found in Somali waters is the stonefish, which looks like a piece of coral but has a poisonous venom.

GOING FOR GOLD

In recent decades, the country has become very involved in sports. Somalia has been a member of the International Athletics Federation since 1959, and since 1972, many Somalis have competed in the Olympics. In the 2004 Summer Olympics in Athens, Fartun Abukar Omar and Abdulla Mohamed Hussein represented Somalia in women's and men's races, respectively. Although Somalia has competed enthusiastically in five Olympic games, it has yet to take home a medal.

A Somali athlete named Abdi Bile won the first gold medal for his country in the 1987 World Athletic Championships in Rome. Many good athletes leave Somalia to train abroad, since facilities in other countries are better. Somali-born Olympic runner Abdihakem Abdirahman is one such athlete. Now an American citizen, he competed in the 2004 Summer Olympics and finished twelfth in the 10,000 meter (6.21 mile) race.

Mogadishu has a large stadium for soccer games and other sports. Soccer, the world's most popular sport, is also ardently followed in Somalia,

A group of Somali boys playing soccer, or football as they prefer to call it.

THE STARRY AFRICAN NIGHT

For centuries, Somalis have been intrigued by the stars in the sky and spend hours gazing at them. In most of Somalia, there is an absence of brightly lit tall buildings and air pollution that cloud the sky.

The nomads in the vast open countryside, especially, have an incredible view of a dark sky pitted with millions of bright stars. Many Somalis have gone into careers in astronomy and astrology, and a Somali named Musa Galaal wrote a book called *The Terminology and Practice of Weather Lore, Astronomy and Astrology*, which brought him international fame.

Somalis enjoyed gazing at the stars during their leisure time. They also planned important events in their life according to the movements of the stars and the moon. For instance, some Somalis would consult an astrologer before planning a wedding or an important trip. If the astrologer predicted that the chosen day would be an unlucky one, the Somali would change the date of the event. Somalis also believed a boy to be especially blessed if he were born during the new moon.

both as a participatory and as a spectator sport. Other favorite games that Somalis play include volleyball and several water sports. American football and boxing also attract good spectator crowds.

CURTAILED CITY PLEASURES

During their brief dominance of Somalia from mid-2006, the Islamic Courts imposed Islamic law (Sharia law) on the territory it oversaw. As a result, most forms of entertainment—movies, music, television, and videos, which were perceived to be endorsing immorality—were banned.

The cities still come alive at night, however, when men and women dress up for an evening out on the town. Although popular bars, discos, and other nightspots in Mogadishu are no longer patronized, Somalis find entertainment in restaurants and cafés, indulging in lively conversations over a meal or a cup of coffee.

Apart from going to cafés and restaurants, Mogadishu residents also enjoy watching plays or going to poetry readings. Although the well-known Mogadishu National Theater is now largely ruined, Somalis still support the arts by going to smaller venues.

A few years ago, going to the movies to see an American or European film on the weekends was commonplace. Today these cinemas have been shut down. UIC gunmen are known to have stormed into packed movie houses to arrest and punish Somalis for ignoring the decree prohibiting such entertainments.

RURAL ENTERTAINMENT

Nomads and other inhabitants of rural Somalia have their own traditional entertainment. The men have activities that tend to be different from the women's. They enjoy working in groups—caring for their flocks, raising crops, or hunting for food. Women enjoy visiting one another and cooking meals together or making handicrafts. A daily trip to the market is a favorite activity.

An afternoon nap, or a siesta, is almost customary for men and women alike, in both rural and urban areas. Somalis close their shops, leave their fields, or stop cooking when the siesta hour comes around. This downtime typically lasts from 2:00 to 4.30 P.M.

In the cities, workers often leave their offices and go home to have a meal and a rest, then return for a few more hours of work.

FESTIVALS

FESTIVALS ARE JOYOUS OCCASIONS in Somalia in which family, friends, and clan members gather together for feasts and merrymaking. Nearly all festivities have a religious significance, whether it is to celebrate a birth or marriage or to observe a public event.

The Islamic lunar calendar dictates the dates of Islamic festivals in Somalia, as is also true in all other Muslim nations. Somalis celebrate the new year of the Islamic calendar with a festival called Muharram. During the first 10 days of the first month, three things are done: all Muslim Somalis tell the tale of the "Tree at the Boundary," while Shiite Muslims honor the Prophet Muhammad's grandson Hussein and celebrate Ashura.

Other important celebrations are Maulid an-Nabi (MAU-lid ahn-NAH-bee) and Ramadan. Maulid an-Nabi occurs on the 12th day of the third month, and Ramadan is observed throughout the ninth month.

Left: **Somali dancers moving rhythmically with great passion in a performance.**

Opposite: **Somalis parading with their national flag, raised in a public display of nationalistic fervor.**

CALENDAR OF SOMALI HOLIDAYS

National Holidays

January 1	New Year's Day
May 1	Labor Day
June 26	Independence of Somaliland
July 1	Independence of the Somali Republic

Religious Holidays

Month 1, days 1–10	Muharram
Month 1, day 1	The Tree at the Boundary
Month 1, days 1–9	Oh Hussein! Oh Hussein!
Month 1, day 10	Ashura
Month 3, day 12	Prophet Muhammad's Birthday (Maulid an-Nabi)
Month 9	Ramadan
Month 10, day 1	Eid al-Fitr
Month 12, day 10	Eid al-Adha

Christian Holidays

March/April	Easter
December 25	Christmas

MUHARRAM

Muslims believe that on the first day of Muharram an angel shakes a tree growing at the boundary of earth and paradise. The tree represents the Muslim people, and each leaf represents an individual. The Somalis believe that if a leaf bearing an individual's name falls off, that person will die during the coming year.

Because the angel is the only being to see each falling leaf, no one knows whose time will have come until the person actually dies. Therefore, when anyone dies, Somalis believe that the angel had shaken that person's leaf off the tree on the first day of Muharram.

"OH HUSSEIN! OH HUSSEIN!" The Prophet Muhammad had a grandson named Hussein who was killed in battle. The Muslims recount the story

of his life and death every night during the first 10 days of Muharram. Often, Somalis will shout, "Oh Hussein! Oh Hussein!" as they listen to their religious leaders telling the highly emotional story. For this reason, this annual honoring of the Prophet's grandson has come to be known as "Oh Hussein! Oh Hussein!"

During the daylight hours of Muharram, Somalis will honor Hussein by reenacting important events in his life exactly as has been recorded in history.

DAY OF ASHURA The 10th day of Muharram is called Ashura. This festival, which is observed by the Shia community, represents the end of the mourning period for Hussein. For Sunni Muslims, Ashura is the beginning of celebrations for the perpetuation of humankind, as represented by the saving of Noah and his family during the 40 days of the deluge. Somali children in particular are fond of listening to this account of Noah and the great flood.

Muslims, like Christians and Jews, believe that God directed Noah to build an ark, and that Noah was then told to bring two specimens of every bird and beast, male and female, into his ark. In this way, Noah's family and the birds and beasts of the earth were kept alive during the deluge that destroyed the rest of humankind. On the day of Ashura, Shia Somali men reenact the death of Hussein. At nightfall everyone in the neighborhood gathers to attend a feast.

Shiite Muslims look forward to Ashura, when they will hear again the story of Noah and the great flood.

The festival of fire, Neeroosh or Dab-shid, marks the beginning of the Somali solar year. During this time, Somalis build bonfires, perform stick fights, and dance.

BIRTHDAY OF THE PROPHET

On the 12th day of the third month of the Islamic calendar, Somalis celebrate the birth of the Prophet Muhammad. The village or the family gathers together to listen to stories and legends about this special event.

According to legend, 7,000 angels brought heavenly mist to earth inside a golden urn. This urn was presented to Muhammad's mother while in labor with her son. As the baby appeared, every living creature proclaimed, "There is no God but Allah, and Muhammad is His Prophet." The angels then bathed the newborn Muhammad in the heavenly mist.

HOLY MONTH OF RAMADAN

Muslims all over the world observe a month of fasting during Ramadan, the ninth month of the Islamic calendar. Somali Muslims take no food or liquid from dawn to dusk throughout the month.

Muslims firmly believe in fasting as a means by which they can truly show their devotion to Allah and to Muhammad. They believe it builds self-discipline and enables them to show compassion to the less fortunate.

Since Ramadan is determined by the Muslim lunar calendar, it takes place at a somewhat different time every year. If Somalis have to fast during a cool rainy period, they find it fairly tolerable. But during a hot dry period, they have a tough time spending an entire day without water.

EID AL-FITR On the last day of Ramadan, after worship and prayers, Muslims end their fast. The festival that follows is called Eid al-Fitr (EED-AHL-fitr) and lasts for three days. All Somalis celebrate by feasting and visiting friends and family. They get together to socialize and to give gifts to children and the poor.

Wealthy urban Somalis usually invite their friends and families to their homes for feasts, while rural Somalis feast with other village members or townsfolk who have come home for the holiday.

EID AL-ADHA

The last Muslim holiday during the lunar year is called Eid al-Adha (EED AHL-ad-ah). On this day, Somali Muslims remember how Abraham nearly sacrificed his first son, celebrating the event as signifying Abraham's faith and love for Allah.

They tell of how Allah told Abraham to prove his devotion by sacrificing his beloved son. It was heartbreaking for Abraham, but he was prepared to do God's bidding. At the very moment that he was raising the knife to kill Ishmael, an angel bade him to stop. This was because Abraham had already shown his devotion to Allah by being willing to carry out the act.

Abraham then slaughtered a sheep and offered it as a sacrifice in place of what was to have been his son. On Id al-Adha, Somali Muslims visit the graves of their relatives and, for those who can afford to sacrifice an animal, distribute the slaughtered meat and other food to the less fortunate.

117

A ritual called robdoon (ROB-doon) is performed in times of drought. Religious leaders read from the Koran and ask Allah to send rain.

THREE-DAY WEDDINGS

Wedding festivities may last for three days in Somalia, especially if the family of the bride can afford such a party. For three days and three nights before the wedding ceremony, friends and family members visit the bride's home for dancing and feasting.

The first two days and nights of wedding celebrations are attended mostly by the younger generation, but on the last night, everyone concerned will be there, and the dancing goes on until midnight. When it is time for the newlyweds to depart to start their new life together, the bride leaves the party with an older woman who helps her shower and put on new clothes. If the couple is well-off, they then drive off to another city for their honeymoon. All the guests follow them in cars to a halfway point in their journey. At this midpoint, all the guests get out of their cars and dance and sing into the early hours of the morning.

At weddings, merry-making and dancing often go on until late at night.

CIRCUMCISION CEREMONIES

Both male and female Somali children are circumcised. Circumcision is viewed as a rite of passage, and festivities surround these rituals. The parents invite all their friends, relatives, and neighbors for a feast after the child's circumcision ceremony. To prepare for this feast, the women of the household will cook all night, having killed as many animals as is necessary.

A young girl who has to undergo the ordeal of circumcision must first take a shower. The women in her family prepare for the ceremony by wrapping old scarves around their shoulders and shaving their heads. A religious leader then reads out parts of the Koran, and the circumcision takes place.

After that people come into the house in small groups to partake of the food and to fumigate their hair with incense smoke. Others wait outside, singing and dancing until it is their turn to enter the house.

There is a growing movement in Somalia and other Muslim countries to renounce female circumcision, or female genital mutilation (FGM) as it is usually now called. This issue was highlighted in this book's earlier chapter, "Lifestyle."

Everyone in this group is likely to have been circumcised. Feasts and celebrations are held to commemorate the event, but circumcision is a painful ordeal for the young girls of Somalia.

119

FOOD

THE STAPLES OF THE Somali diet are rice, pasta, bananas, and the meat of sheep or goats. Corn and beans are also grown and eaten.

Because parts of the country came under Italian rule, many Somalis eat pasta, such as spaghetti and macaroni, as a staple. The local bread of Somalia is called *muufo* (moo-OO-foh), which is a flat bread similar to pita bread but is made with cornmeal.

The nomadic groups raise sheep, goats, and cattle to sell, but they also depend on these animals as a source of their own food. That was why these nomads suffered so greatly during the terrible years of famine in Somalia between the late 1970s and early 1990s. Not only was their means of livelihood lost when their animals died during droughts and floods, but meat and milk from their cattle were no longer available to them.

Above: **Somalis were forced to live on hand-outs during the famine of the 1990s.**

Opposite: **Children eating from a communal dish, using only the right hand.**

Somalis also eat the meat of camels, which they consider to be a delicacy. A Somali family serves camel meat at a meal only if they are expecting important guests. Pork is a meat that is enjoyed by most Westerners but which Somalis will not eat or even touch, as the Koran forbids it.

Cooking outdoors is widely practiced in villages in Somalia.

SOMALI KITCHENS

In many areas of Somalia, kitchens often have no running water or electricity. Urban kitchens in city areas are equipped with every convenience and electronic appliances. But as a result of the civil wars of the 1990s, even homes in the cities lost access to electricity and running water. Circumstances forced people to prepare food with contaminated water, which resulted in serious illnesses and many deaths.

In the countryside many homes do not have a kitchen. Rural living quarters are usually big enough for only a few beds. This is especially true of the nomads, whose mobile shelters serve only as sleeping quarters.

Rural Somalis prepare their food outdoors, or inside a central village hut. Village women often gather together to prepare corn or sorghum porridge in the mornings. They set up a tin bucket, add the corn or sorghum and water, and pound the mixture with a stick.

In contrast, there are well-off urban Somalis who have been unaffected by the civil wars. This small privileged group has modern kitchens and, often, even employs cooks to prepare the family meals. Apart from the cooking, these cooks usually do the marketing and serve the food.

WHY SOMALIS FAST

The fourth pillar of Islam requires its followers to observe Ramadan by fasting during daylight hours. People of other religions sometimes find it difficult to understand the significance of the strict fast.

Muslims have several reasons to refrain from food and water during Ramadan. In addition to enabling them to demonstrate their love and devotion to Allah, Somali Muslims believe that fasting helps them to clear their minds to focus on religion, family, and personal goals.

They also believe that fasting allows them to develop a deeper compassion for all those who do not have enough food to eat.

In recent times, when extended periods of food shortages and famines afflicted most of the people, many Somalis did not have to fast cermonially to know exactly how it felt to go without food for days and even weeks on end.

This array of grains and spices is the merchandise a local market stall has to offer.

Women cooking in an indoor kitchen. Preparing a meal often brings women together for enjoyable socializing.

TIME FOR FEASTS

At the end of Ramadan, Somalis express their joy by feasting. Food is usually plentiful at such times, with generous servings of meat, vegetables, homemade bread, and rice. Friends, families, neighbors, and the poor are invited to the feasts.

Somalis also eat well on other festivals, birthdays, weddings, and circumcisions. Amid the general feasting, there will be dancing and storytelling as well as singing.

Preparing for these feasts is an enjoyable experience for Somali women. They make a trip to the local market and buy the food they need, perhaps even adding one or two handicrafts to their baskets for decorations. A market may have hundreds of stalls selling fruits, vegetables, meat, rice, bread, coffee, tea, and milk.

The vendors who sell charcoal at these colorful markets are well patronized, as most rural Somali women cook using charcoal for fuel.

SOMALI MEALTIME

It is customary for Somali men and women to eat separately. The women prepare the food and serve the men, and only after the menfolk have finished will the women sit down to eat with the children. Even in the cities it was not the accepted practice for women to eat together with men in restaurants until the late 1990s. Women and girls prepare the

TABLE MANNERS

When Somalis are about to eat a meal, they first wash their hands in a large bowl of soapy water. For a family meal in the rural areas, the father sits down and serves himself by reaching into the serving bowl with a spoon or with his right hand.

Next, the children help themselves. If their mother is sitting down to eat with them, she serves herself first and then her sons. She uses her right hand or a serving spoon to ladle out the food.

Rural Somalis often eat with their fingers, and this is not

considered ill-mannered. When picking up food with their right hand, Somalis use only the first three fingers. When rural Somalis venture into the cities, they have a difficult time trying to eat with a knife and fork. Urbanized Somalis are more used to the Western style of eating, but even in the cities, people commonly eat with their fingers.

Many African Muslims, including the Somalis, believe that for a meal to be truly enjoyed, it has to be eaten in this manner. The left hand is never used for eating, as this is the "unclean" hand in the Muslim tradition, the one that Muslims use for toilet ablutions and that is never used to bring food to the mouth.

meals together in rural areas. If meat is going to be on the table, then the young boys of the family are often sent out to pick out the sheep or goat to be slaughtered.

Everyone gathers together once the meal is ready, sitting at a big table to eat. After the meal the older boys and girls of the village often collect wood to build a bonfire. Then they will dance together around the fire. The fire not only provides light but also keeps away flies and mosquitoes. For the youngsters, such enjoyable campfire activities are as much a part of the meal as the eating itself.

A Somali butcher at work in an open-air market.

EATING OUT

The cities of Somalia offer a wide variety of food in their restaurants. Fancy restaurants are inexpensive by Western standards.

A good three-course meal costs about $10 per person. A meal at the cheapest restaurants costs between $2 and $5. An even better value is the food from street vendors, which can be bought fresh and hot for less than $2. Although such prices seem cheap to the people of developed nations, the value of the Somali shilling is rather low, so that only a few U.S. dollars can represent a lot of money to a Somali.

During the month of Ramadan, almost all restaurants in Somalia remain closed until sundown. The few restaurants that remain open during the day are usually owned by non-Muslims.

Some of the restaurants in the big cities, especially in Mogadishu, offer cuisines from other countries, such as Chinese, Italian, Middle Eastern, European, and even American-style foods. Some Mogadishu restaurants and those in other coastal cities offer fresh fish and lobster caught by Somali fishermen that very day.

Because of the strong Arabic influence after the seventh century, many of the city restaurants sell traditional Arabic food such as kebabs (skewers of grilled lamb and vegetables).

REGIONAL FOOD

People in each of the four regions of Somalia tend to favor their own local produce, which is more readily available to them and is cheaper.

Those along the coast eat a lot of fresh fish, while the nomads eat the meat of sheep, goats, and cattle, and rarely have fish. Somalis living by the rivers have fresh vegetables and maybe even crocodile meat.

When Somalis have a chance to eat well, they do not stint on food. On occasions that call for a feast, there will be plenty of dishes on the table—several kinds of meat and vegetables, pasta, rice, and bread.

Muufo is the most popular bread among Somalis. Many Somalis make a living baking it and wholesaling it to market stallholders and others. The corn for *muufo* is first ground into flour, then yeast, salt, oil, and water are added. The dough is slapped repeatedly until it is fairly flat, then placed in a clay oven over hot coals. Once the bread is done, the baker reaches a hand into an aperture in the oven to pull out the loaf.

For this reason, Somalis who make *muufo* often have trademark burns and scars on their arms and hands.

Street vendors selling the favorite Somali bread called *muufo,* which resembles pita bread.

One favorite breakfast dish is fried sheep or goat's liver with onions and bread. On a rare occasion, they will cook camel's liver. The fatty hump of the camel is also considered a delicacy.

Somalis are very fond of marinara sauce, which is of Italian origin and made of tomatoes, onions, garlic, and spices. The sauce was a coveted food item during the famine years, and families considered themselves well-fed if they could afford a can of marinara sauce to eat with pasta once a week. The other Italian influenced food item is pasta. A big amount of spaghetti, known as *baasto*, is another popular food consumed by the people.

THE VERSATILITY OF MILK

For many rural Somalis, milk is an important staple food. Nomadic herdsmen may drink up to 9 liters (2.37 gallons) of milk a day.

For Somalis, camel milk and its by-products are an important source of protein, calcium, and vitamins. Milk is usually stored in a covered pitcher or wooden bucket. Fresh milk will usually keep for a few days even with the scorching temperatures.

Somalis also churn milk to make butter. This butter, when cooked over low heat will turn into ghee (G-ee), otherwise known as clarified butter, which has a somewhat nutty aroma.

The Rahanweyn clan of south Somalia considers coffee beans cooked in ghee a delicacy. Ghee can keep for a few months if stored in a *tabut* (TA-boot) which is a leather container.

When camel milk is fermented for a month, *jinow* (GEE-no), a product resembling a solid yogurt, is produced. To Somalis, the highest expression of hospitality a fellow countryman might offer to someone of importance is by giving the guest milk.

THE CUP THAT REFRESHES

Coffee and tea are Somalis' favorite beverages, and they are often served before or after a meal. This is because some Muslims do not like to mix food and drink.

Somalis prefer to grind their own freshly roasted coffee beans rather than to buy ready-ground ones. They may drink their coffee black or add milk and sugar.

Somalis serve tea in several different ways. One of these ways is to add lots of milk and sugar to produce tea with a thick milky consistency. They also drink their tea plain or add fresh fruit for extra flavor.

Islam forbids its followers from drinking alcoholic beverages, so devout Somali Muslims do not drink alcohol, although there are some Somalis who will take an occasional glass of beer or wine. With urbanization, it is not uncommon to see Somalis in city areas consuming alcohol.

Somalia produces its own rum, which is enjoyed by some Somalis. Visitors who come to Somalia also get a chance to enjoy this local liquor. Generally, Somalis consume a lot of water, especially during the hot months, as well as canned or bottled carbonated drinks.

This man is enjoying his glass of coffee with milk. Somalis love their coffee breaks at any time of day.

129

SOMALI CRABMEAT STEW

This recipe serves four to six.

2 cups white rice
5 cups water
¼ cup peanut oil (can be substituted with butter)
1 cup onions, finely chopped
1 teaspoon curry powder
1 teaspoon grated ginger
1 teaspoon salt
1 teaspoon crushed red pepper flakes
1 pound tomatoes, cut into small chunks
2 pounds crabmeat (other seafood, such as scallops, can be substituted)

In a pot, wash and rinse the rice. Drain, then add five cups of water. Cover the pot and bring the water to a boil over high heat. Reduce the heat and let the rice simmer for 15 to 20 minutes or until done. Set aside.

To prepare the stew, heat the peanut oil in a heavy saucepan. Sauté the onions, curry powder, ginger, salt, and red pepper flakes until the onions are lightly browned.

Add the tomatoes and cook until soft. Add the crabmeat (or other seafood) and sauté for another ten minutes.

Garnish as desired and serve with the cooked rice.

BASBOUSA (SEMOLINA CAKE)

This recipe serves four.

¾ cup sugar

1¼ cups buttermilk

2 cups semolina

1½ teaspoons vanilla extract

1 tablespoon baking powder

1½ teaspoons baking soda

¾ cup melted butter or margarine

1 cup sugar

1 cup water

½ lemon, juiced

In a large bowl, combine the sugar and buttermilk. In another bowl, combine the semolina, vanilla extract, baking powder, and baking soda. Carefully add the semolina mixture to the buttermilk mixture. Mix well, then fold in the melted butter.

Pour mixture into a well-greased 11-by-7-inch rectangle baking pan or a round pan and let it sit for 20 minutes. Bake in a preheated oven of 350°F (180°C) for 30 minutes.

In the meantime, combine sugar, water, and lemon juice in a saucepan. Bring the mixture to a boil. Reduce the heat and simmer for 25 to 30 minutes. Let the syrup cool and thicken.

To serve, drizzle syrup over warm slices of cake. Top off with raisins, dried fruits, or almonds, if desired.

MAP OF SOMALIA

ECONOMIC SOMALIA

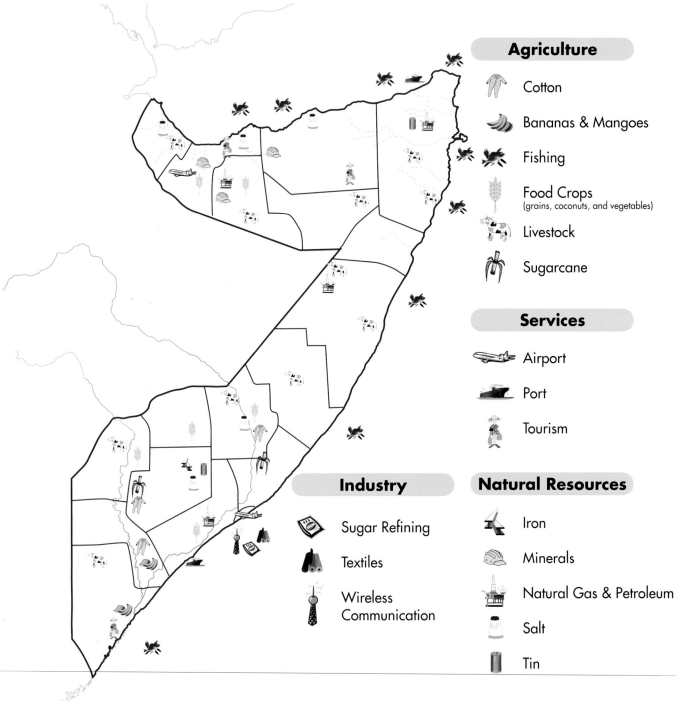

Agriculture

- Cotton
- Bananas & Mangoes
- Fishing
- Food Crops (grains, coconuts, and vegetables)
- Livestock
- Sugarcane

Services

- Airport
- Port
- Tourism

Industry

- Sugar Refining
- Textiles
- Wireless Communication

Natural Resources

- Iron
- Minerals
- Natural Gas & Petroleum
- Salt
- Tin

ABOUT THE ECONOMY

OVERVIEW

Somalia's economic status remains that of a Third World country. Its few natural resources are largely unexploited. The previous centrally planned economy was gradually replaced by a free market one. The basis of its economy remains rooted in agriculture and animal herding. Remittances from Somalis working abroad, amounting to about $2 billion annually, also contribute to Somalia's economy. Somalia has a small fishing industry in the north, and a few light industries in the south. They are mostly based on the processing of agricultural products. Electricity and telecommunications industries are privately owned and operated.

GROSS DOMESTIC PRODUCT (GDP)

$5.023 billion (2006 estimate)

GDP GROWTH

2.6 percent (2006 estimate)

LAND USE

Arable land: 1.64 percent; permanent crops: 0.04 percent; others: 98.32 percent (2005 estimates)

CURRENCY

1 Somali shilling (SOS) = 100 centesimi
Notes: 1,000; 500; 100; 50; 20; 10; 5 SOS
Coins: 100; 50; 25; 10; 5 centesimi
1 USD = 1,473.03 SOS (October 2006)

NATURAL RESOURCES

Uranium, iron ore, tin, gypsum, manganese, copper, salt, natural gas, and petroleum

AGRICULTURAL PRODUCTS

Bananas, sugarcane, mangoes, sorghum, corn, coconut, rice, sesame seeds, beans, cattle, sheep, goats, fish

INDUSTRIES

Sugar refining, textiles, wireless communication

MAJOR EXPORTS

Livestock, bananas, hides, fish, charcoal, scrap metal

MAJOR IMPORTS

Manufactured goods, petroleum products, foodstuffs, construction materials, khat (qat or jaad)

TRADE PARTNERS

United Arab Emirates, Yemen, Oman, Djibouti, Kenya, India, Brazil.

EXTERNAL DEBT

$3 billion (2001 estimate)

TELECOMMUNICATIONS

Internet users: 90,000; main telephone lines: 100,000; mobile telephone lines: 500,000 (2005 estimates)

AIRPORTS

65; 7 with paved runways, 58 unpaved

WORKFORCE

3.7 million

CULTURAL SOMALIA

Garoowe
The capital city of Puntland. It has transformed from a small rural town to a busy trading city. The regional government, ministries, and the presidential palace are located here.

Galdogob
A metropolitan border town, it is one of the most peaceful regions in Somalia. Its thriving livestock industry makes it a great spot to watch local and visiting merchants from Addis Ababa, Djibouti, and Dire Dawa congregate and conduct their daily business.

Mogadishu
Somalia's capital city is rich with history. The old city, Hammawein, was one of the most scenic spots on the African coast, but civil war has lain to ruins most of its attractions. Some remaining ones are the Arba Rucun Mosque (Mosque of the four pillars), the Fakr al-Din mosque, the Bakara Market, as well as Arab-style and Italian-inspired architecture.

Merca
A small region with a lovely old Arab town feel. Swimming in the warm, clear water at Sinbusi Beach is popular as sandbanks keep the sharks at bay.

Gendershe
Narrow streets, old tombs, and mosques define this historic coastal village. It is also home to one of the best white sand beaches in Africa.

Kismaayo
Part of Jubaland, the region was founded by the sultan of Zanzibar in 1872. The town is known for its beautiful palace and mosques built by the sultan.

ABOUT
THE CULTURE

OFFICIAL NAME
Somalia

FLAG DESCRIPTION
Light blue (influenced by the flag of the UN), with a large five-pointed star in the center

CAPITAL
Mogadishu

POPULATION
8.86 million (2006 estimate)

ETHNIC GROUPS
Somali 85 percent, Bantu and other non-Somali (including Arabs) 15 percent

RELIGIOUS GROUPS
Sunni Muslim 99 percent, Shiite Muslim and Christian less than one percent

BIRTH RATE
34.53 births/1,000 population (2006 estimate)

DEATH RATE
16.63 deaths/1,000 population (2006 estimate)

LANGUAGES
Somali (official), Arabic, Italian, English

LITERACY RATE
People ages 15 and above who can read and write: 37.8 percent (2005 est.)

NATIONAL HOLIDAYS
Independence of Somaliland (June 26), Foundation of the Somali Republic (July 1), Muharram/Islamic New Year (variable date), The Tree at the Boundary (variable date), Oh Hussein! Oh Hussein! (variable date), Ashura (variable date), Prophet Muhammad's Birthday (variable date), Id al-Fitr (variable date), Id al-Adha (variable date)

LEADERS IN POLITICS
Aden Abdullah Osman—first president of independent Somalia (1960–67)
Abdi Rashid Ali Shermarke—first prime minister of independent Somalia (1960–64) and then president (1967–69)
Mohammed Siad Barre—president of socialist Somalia (1969–91)
Abdulkassim Salat Hassan—president of Transitional National Government (2000–04)
Ali Khalif Gelayadh—prime minister of Transitional National Government (2000–01)
Dahir Riyale Kahin—president of Somaliland (2002–)
Abdullahi Yusuf—president of Somalia Transitional Federal Government (2004–)
Ali Mohammed Ghedi—prime minister of Somalia Transitional Federal Government (2004–)

TIME LINE

IN SOMALIA	IN THE WORLD
100 B.C.	**116–17 B.C.**
Based on the history of Eastern Cushitic language, it is believed that people from around Lake Tana, Ethiopia, migrated to southern Somalia, and are the ancestors of Early Somalis.	The Roman Empire reaches its greatest extent, under Emperor Trajan (98–17).
A.D. 100	
Population growth; Somalis move from south to north.	
A.D. 600	**A.D. 600**
Muslims from Saudi Arabia migrate to Somalia and Horn of Africa. They establish the sultanate of Adel and settle along the Gulf of Aden.	Height of the Mayan civilization
	1530
	Beginning of transatlantic slave trade organized by the Portuguese in Africa
	1620
	Pilgrims sail the *Mayflower* to America.
	1776
1839	U.S. Declaration of Independence
Britain enters into two treaties with Somali sultanates to supply cattle to Somalia.	
1860s	**1861**
France controls Somali coast; French Somaliland	The U.S. Civil War begins.
1869–84	**1869**
Egyptians occupy northeastern coastal towns; British oust them and sign treaties with Somali clans; British Somaliland formed.	The Suez Canal is opened.
1891–94	
Colonial boundaries drawn for British Somaliland and Italian Somaliland; Somalis excluded from negotiations	**1914**
	World War I begins.
1940–41	**1939**
Italians occupy British Somaliland; British occupy Italian Somaliland.	World War II begins.
	1945
	The United States drops atomic bombs on Hiroshima and Nagasaki.
	1949
1960	The North Atlantic Treaty Organization (NATO) is formed.
Independent Republic of Somalia is formed.	

IN SOMALIA	IN THE WORLD
1969–70 Siad Barre overthrows interim government; Communist governance. French Somaliland becomes Republic of Djibouti.	**1966–69** The Chinese Cultural Revolution
1972 Standardized script for Somali language.	
1974–75 Severe drought; starvation and refugees.	**1986** Nuclear power disaster at Chernobyl in Ukraine
1990–91 Siad Barre flees Mogadishu. Northern region self-declares as Republic of Somaliland; famine and civil war rages.	**1991** Breakup of the Soviet Union
1992–95 UN and U.S. troops arrive to restore order; attempt unsuccessful; troops leave.	
1998 Puntland and Jubaland regions declare autonomy.	**1997** Hong Kong is returned to China.
2000–03 Interim government created, recognized only by international community and not by Somaliland, Puntland, and various southern Somali warlords; in-fighting and civil wars occur.	**2001** Terrorists crash planes in New York, Washington, D.C., and Pennsylvania. **2003** War in Iraq begins.
2004 Transitional Federal Government (TFG) and Somalia Transitional Federal Institutions (TFI) created; a tsunami off Indonesia hits Somali coast, killing hundreds, displacing thousands.	
Jun–Jul 2006 Union of Islamic Courts (UIC) seize Mogadishu and southern Somalia.	
Nov–Dec 2006 UIC and TFG fail to meet for peace talks. UIC assaults TFG stronghold in Baidoa but loses to Ethiopian-backed government troops; abandons Mogadishu.	
Jan 2007 UIC retreats and leaves Kismaayo.	

GLOSSARY

akal (ah-KAHL)
Nomadic homes of hides and flexible sticks.

arish (AH-reesh)
Rectangular home built of timber, mud, dung, and straw, with pitched tin or thatched roof.

baraca (bah-RAH-kah)
Rectangular home with cement floors and timber walls.

baruka (bah-ROO-kah)
Power, which is supposedly God-given, to bless or curse others.

Candho-qoy (KAHN-doh-koy)
Literally, "the place of moist udders" of the camel.

casa matoni (KAH-sa mah-TOH-nee)
A *baraca* with stone or cement walls.

casa moro (KAH-sa MOH-roh)
A two-story stone home built in an Arab style.

dik-dik
Small antelope that lives in northern Somalia and along the major rivers.

gabaye (gah-bah-YAH)
A poem composed to convey to a community important decisions made by tribal leaders.

geel-weyta (GEEL-WEY-tah)
Literally "the place that weakens animals."

guntina (goon-TEE-nah)
Long colorful cloth that Somali women wrap around their bodies to form a garment.

Haud
Geographic region extending across the width of Somalia from Hargeysa in the north to Gaalkacyo in the south, with lush vegetation during the rainy seasons.

hoopoe
Pinkish-brown bird with black and white stripes, native to Somalia.

jaad (or khat or qat)
Leaf of this plant is chewed to achieve a mildly euphoric and stimulating effect.

laylis (LAH-yis)
Exercises in a school textbook, known as "breaking of a young camel."

muufo (moo-OO-foh)
Somali bread, a flat bread resembling pita.

raadra (RAAH-drah)
Conduct research; literally, "to trace lost animals."

saari (SAAH-ri)
Island

zar (zahr)
Evil spirit supposedly invading the souls of women who harbor grievances against their husbands.

FURTHER INFORMATION

BOOKS

Abdullahi, Mohamed Diriye. *Culture and Customs of Somalia*. Westport, CT: Greenwood Press, 2001.

Bowden, Mark. *Black Hawk Down*. London: Corgi, 2000.

Burnett, John S. *Where Soldiers Fear to Tread: A Relief Worker's Tale of Survival*. New York: Bantam Books, 2005.

Farah, Nuruddin. *Maps*. New York: Penguin Books, 2000.

————. *Yesterday, Tomorrow: Voices from the Somali Diaspora*. London: Cassell, 2000.

Hoffman, Mary. *The Color of Home*. London: Frances Lincoln, 2005.

Stanton, Martin. *Somalia on $5 a Day: A Soldier's Story*. New York: Ballantine Books, 2003.

Nnoromele, Salome C. *Somalia*. San Diego: Lucent Books, 2000.

Peterson, Scott. *Me Against My Brother: At War in Somalia, Sudan and Rwanda—A Journalist Reports from the Battlefields of Africa*. New York: Routledge, 2001.

WEB SITES

Arab Net: Somalia. www.arab.net/somalia

Central Intelligence Agency World Factbook (select Somalia from country list). www.cia.gov/cia/publications/factbook

Lonely Planet World Guide: Somalia. www.lonelyplanet.com/worldguide/destinations/africa/somalia

Somaliland Republic Country Profile. www.somalilandnet.com/slandhome.shtml

U.S Department of State: Somalia. www.state.gov/r/pa/ei/bgn/2863.htm

FILM

Black Hawk Down. Sony Pictures Home Entertainment, 2006.

MUSIC

Dusty Foot Philosopher, The. K'Naan. Track and Field, Inc., 2005.

Jamiila: Songs from a Somali City. Jamiila. Original Music, 1995.

Journey, The. Maryam Mursal. Real World, 1998.

New Dawn. Waaberi. Real World, 1997.

BIBLIOGRAPHY

Barnes, Virginia Lee. *Aman: The Story of a Somali Girl*. New York: Pantheon Books, 1994.

Godbeer, Deardre. *Somalia*. New York: Chelsea House, 1988.

Henze, Paul B. *The Horn of Africa*. London: MacMillan, 1991.

Hodd, Michael (editor). *East African Handbook*. Chicago: Passport Books, 1995.

Hudson, Peter. *A Leaf in the Wind: Travels in Africa*. New York: Walker and Company, 1988.

Laitan, David D., and Said S. Samatar. *Somalia: Nation in Search of a State*. Boulder, CO: Westview Press, 1987.

Lewis, I. M. *The Modern History of Somaliland*. New York: Frederick A. Praeger, 1965.

Nelson, Harold D. (editor). *Somalia: A Country Study*. Washington, DC: American University Press, Foreign Area Studies, 1982.

Sahnoun, Mohamed. *Somalia: The Missed Opportunities*. Washington, DC: United States Institute of Peace Press, 1994.

IRIN News Org: UN Office for the Coordination of Humanitarian Affairs. www.irinnews.org

Official Federal Government Website for Somalia. www.somali-gov.info

Somalia News. www.somalianews.com

Somalia Online. www.somaliaonline.com

UN Somalia. www.un-somalia.org

INDEX